SHELVE

Scandinavian Lifestyle Habits

Andrew William James

CONTENTS

Introduction

Life these days can be fast and complicated. Many of us are looking for a way to slow down and live a simpler life.

With a bewildering array of lifestyle choices and methods available, it is therefore not surprising that there is confusion over which to choose and how to achieve the ultimate goal of happiness and well-being.

The SHELVE methodology is based on my own experiences and is a collection of what has and hasn't worked for me.

I have been a lifelong follower of simple slow living and in the last fifteen years discovered Scandinavian practices such as Hygge and Lagom.

This book is written for others who are looking for a framework based on popular tried and tested ideas and tools so they can start their journey to achieving happiness and wellbeing.

Part 1

What is SHELVE and how to use this book

"Life is a journey and it's about growing and changing and coming to terms with who you are and loving who and what you are."

Kelly McGillis

There is an old saying that the greatest pleasures in life are the simplest ones.

I certainly believe this to be true and this book aims to share with you the lessons I have learnt, how we are all different and how simplifying our lives can lead to happiness and wellbeing, with what we have and who we are.

Unfortunately, there is no quick route, and I certainly wouldn't expect the reader of this book to adopt every suggestion I make, rather, it would be better to take away suggestions for adaptation to your journey.

All too often we strive for something that simply doesn't exist. This is in part due to marketing or peer pressure. If we buy a certain car, television, clothes or food we will be happy and content. We are told what we should eat to be healthy and if that doesn't work, we can look at skincare products, gyms, magic slimming pills or vitamin tablets.

Over several years, I have read and taken interest in a number of subjects:

- Simple living
- Slow Living
- Minimalism
- Maximalism
- Hygge

- Lagom
- Healthy Eating
- Numerous fad diets
- Various Interior Design Principles
- Quitting Smoking
- Drinking Responsibly
- Personal Finance
- Early Retirement
- Sustainable Living
- Vintage Living

I have to a greater or lesser degree had involvement with all the activities above. What I was looking for was something that combined all these activities rather than choosing from one or the other.

The idea of SHELVE came from taking six key life areas and fusing them with six facilitators, or tools to find a framework that could help people get closer to achieving happiness and wellbeing.

hobbie	**S**	*low*
healt	**H**	ome
hygg	**E**	nvironment
socia	**L**	*agom*
impro	**V**	*intage*
simpl	**E**	conomics

The six key life areas in regular and the six facilitators or tools are in italics.

Interestingly the number six in Feng Shui represents "flow". In certain Chinese cultures, it represents happiness and blessings. Many businesses will display the number six to invite good fortune and wealth. And in numerology the number six signifies domestic happiness, harmony and stability. All of these are principles and beliefs of the SHELVE methodology.

SHELVE is not just a list of six life areas and six facilitators, it is more a fusion of the two and why the categories are broad. Each area has an interdependency on at least one of the facilitators. So, for example Economics, or Finance can be influenced by any of the facilitators, in that, when the basics are right there is space to live a Simple, Slow or Vintage lifestyle. However, a Simple, Slow or Vintage life will help with getting your finances under control. The same is true of Home, once a home is decluttered there is then space to do what you want with it and follow your style.

A representation of SHELVE with all possible interdependencies would look like this:

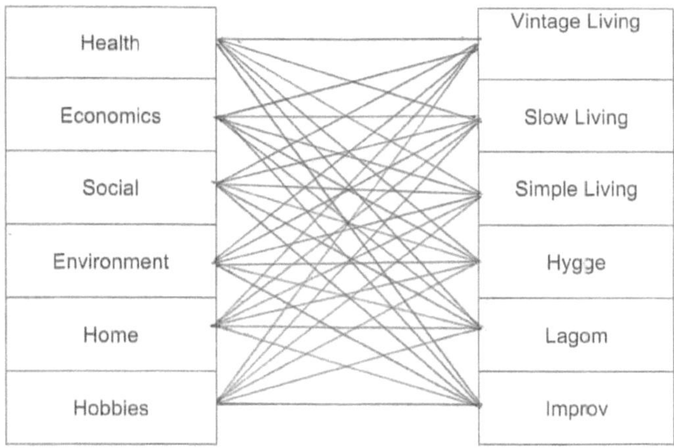

Within each of the Life areas of SHELVE I have included suggestions on how to get the basics right so that, once a good solid foundation is built, you can move on to developing your way of living further.

Throughout this book you will find SHELVE Tips at the end of each section, these are intended either as exercises you may want to follow or as thought provokers. You may find it useful to keep a separate

Journal or use this book as a workbook and record your thoughts in the spaces provided. At the end of this book are templates for your project plan.

This book is divided into five parts. This first part is an introduction to SHELVE. In Part Two we will discuss the various Life Areas, in Part Three the Facilitators and in Part Four we will look at how you can develop your plan, depending on your needs, to improve your happiness and wellbeing.

Part 2

Life Areas

The SHELVE Life Wheel

The SHELVE Life Wheel represents the six Life Areas

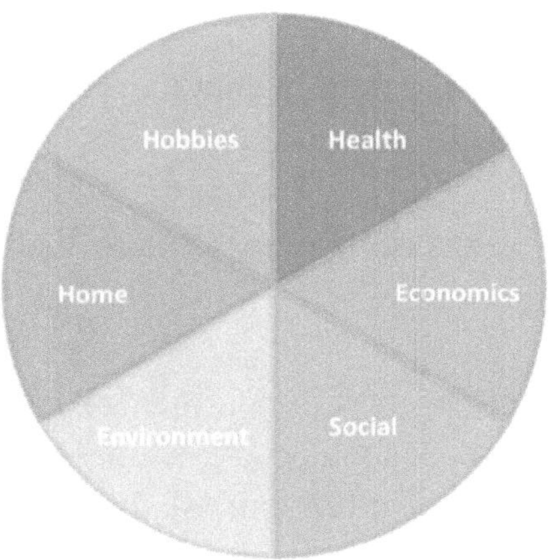

Think of this as the front wheel of a bicycle, without this wheel being as round as possible, it is difficult to steer your way through life.

To find out how happy you are with every area of your life, you may wish to complete a wheel of your own, once you have read this part of the book. Instructions and an example are provided, and it will help you with the fourth part of the book, developing your plan.

Health

"Physical fitness is the first requisite of happiness."

Joseph Pilates

Without good health, we cannot achieve everything we want, and it becomes difficult to focus on improving life.

We are led to believe that Good Health is to look and be physically perfect.

I would argue that this ideal is impossible for most of us to achieve. Good Health is about feeling good about ourselves, having the confidence to achieve our ambitions. It doesn't matter if we don't have perfect bodies, in fact, all that matters is that we feel good, energised and embrace each day as an opportunity to enjoy being alive.

Getting a Good Night's Sleep

"Innocent sleep. Sleep that soothes away all our worries. Sleep that puts each day to rest. Sleep that relieves the weary labourer and heals hurt minds. Sleep, the main course in life's feast, and the most nourishing."

William Shakespeare, Macbeth

Sleep is one of the most important factors to achieving good health, without good sleep we are tired, irritable, and unable to deal effectively with the challenges modern life throws at us.

Recommendations for Adults are seven to nine hours a day of quality sleep. This can of course vary from one individual to another and depends on how active you are during the day, physically or mentally.

A good guide, most people would agree with, is eight hours. Children and Teenagers may need more and older people less. However, find the amount of time that makes you feel good. If you still feel tired the next day, then you need more, if you wake too early then adjust accordingly.

Going to bed and waking up at the same time every morning gives your body clock an all-important routine. If you have a long journey to work, then bed at 10 pm and up at 6 am would be a good schedule. This would allow you time to wind down in the evening before going to sleep and time to enjoy a slow morning routine.

Weekends and Holidays are of course different as the demands on our days are different. Establish a routine that works for you.

Don't forget the Internet is awash with advice on how to get a good night's sleep.

A routine that works for me is:

A good breakfast to start the day gives your body and brain energy. The old saying of breakfast like a King, lunch like a Prince and dinner as a Pauper has some merit. I find an egg on toast with a good decaf coffee makes a great breakfast. Porridge or Oats is another healthy alternative. Lunch can be more elaborate as there is plenty of time in the afternoon to use up the energy in the food. Evening meals tend to be lighter.

Evening meals should be eaten early, if you are eating too late, your body is still trying to process and digest food when it should be winding down ready for sleep. This means you are burning energy and therefore your heart will be pumping faster, blood pressure higher and your body will not be relaxed enough to fall asleep easily.

Limit alcohol when you have work the next day or abstain altogether. This is covered in another chapter in greater detail, however, there is no doubt, too much alcohol in the evening can be detrimental to your health and wellbeing.

Too much of any liquid at night can be a bad thing – even too much water will make you want to get up in the night to visit the bathroom, this interrupts your deep sleep, and you wake up feeling tired and lethargic.

To sleep properly we need to clear out the day's thoughts, relax and enjoy the sensation of feeling tired.

It is important to get into the habit of winding down an hour before bedtime. This could be doing something like keeping a journal and writing down your thoughts for the day or your goals for the next day.

Try and limit the use of electronic devices in that last hour, they tend to stimulate our brains and wake us up. If you end up getting into a WhatsApp or Text conversation it is likely to stimulate your mind and it will be harder to fall asleep. If you can, switch your phone off, one hour before going to bed. Taking it into the bedroom with you and having it on your bedside table will keep a tiny part of your brain alive with thoughts of "will it ring", "will someone text me" or "will I get an email".

Mobile Phones and Cordless Phones emit Electro-Magnetic Waves (EMF), similar to radio waves, the intensity of these waves, nearby, can be quite high. Worryingly no long-term studies are showing the effect of constant exposure to these waves. As a result, there is no clear evidence of whether long-term exposure is harmful or not.

If you must have a phone next to your bed for emergencies, then consider a corded landline.

Bedrooms should be our sanctuaries where at the end of the day we recharge ourselves for the next day.

Ideally, a bedroom should have no electronic devices in it, it should be a calm, simple clean space. I'm not a believer in this one size fits all approach, I like reading or listening to music when I go to bed as this sends me off to sleep. Some people find watching TV in bed sends them off to sleep. I think this may be the case, but the light TVs give off is a blue light which is more likely to interfere with getting a really good deep sleep.

If you live in a noisy area, try going to sleep with a fan on in the background. The noise will help detract from other noises and the gentle whirring may help you fall asleep.

How we wake up is just as important as falling asleep. I've found the best way to wake up, not surprisingly, is slowly.

When we are asleep our hearts and metabolism slow down, so it's important to wake up slowly. Waking up and jumping straight out of bed puts tremendous strain on our bodies and minds. Our minds haven't yet adjusted from sleep to waking, and our bodies are still in slow mode.

Throughout the day it is important you allocate chunks of time to yourself for reflection and to relax. Allocating "me time" first thing in the morning is a great way to prepare yourself mentally and physically for the day ahead.

If your schedule is such that you couldn't possibly find time to have some time to yourself in the morning, then, try setting your alarm earlier.

I used to wake up and listen to the News whilst having a coffee in bed. I did this for several years as I felt it was important to start the day knowing what was happening in the world or if a war had broken out.

For me, this was the wrong way to start the day. The coffee didn't wake me up, it was just a drink and the News or Phone-in Talk shows are always depressing. Something has happened and it is terrible, someone needs to resign, no one can do anything right. At the end of the day, there was nothing I could do, and my life wasn't enriched hearing the latest news first thing in the morning. It only served to start my day on a downer.

Instead of listening to the news and drinking coffee I now drink herbal tea and listen to music. The tea is refreshing and cleansing and the music soothing. This is a much better start to the day, and I don't have to rush as I wake up earlier than I used to. The Vintage Living Person in me prefers to wake up to a 1940s internet radio station and tune into the news later in the day.

You may feel drinking water first thing and Mediation or Pilates are better for you, the key is to find something you do for yourself first thing in the morning and start the day properly. To be avoided is checking email and social media - another good reason not to have your phone in the bedroom.

In summary, the one hour before bed and the first fifteen or so minutes in the morning are the most precious times of the day for our well-being, it gives us a chance to perform a mental reset and take on a new day without feeling fatigued.

SHELVE Tips

For two nights running if you usually have a glass of wine in the evening try drinking herbal tea (Chamomile being the best for sending you to sleep). Switch off your TV, mobile phone, tablet and computer an hour before going to bed and read or listen to music in that time.

When you are ready to go to bed, go to bed and see if you find it easier to sleep and easier to have a proper deep sleep. You may need to repeat this several times during the week as it will take your body and mind time to adjust.

If you still have problems sleeping, try a relaxation exercise. A popular one is to lie down on your bed, then, starting at the top of your body, slowly tense each limb as you gradually work your way down to your toes. Hold the tension for a minute or so and then release the tension in your toes and slowly up to your body until you are completely relaxed.

When waking, set your alarm 15 minutes earlier than your normal time and take time to either sip a glass of water or make yourself a herbal tea and wake up in bed slowly. It may help to have some relaxing music on but avoid the News!

Take these 15 or so minutes as your most precious "me time", enjoy preparing yourself for the day ahead or just let your mind wander.

Physical Exercise

"Take care of your body. It's the only place you have to live in.

Jim Rohn

The key to good health, losing weight and getting a good night's sleep is exercise.

How many times have you joined a gym believing it to be the answer to losing weight? After the initial enthusiasm, you start making excuses, like "I worked late" or "I don't have time today". Walking, Running, Cycling or Swimming are cheaper but are prone to be skipped if you don't make time.

The way to establish a good exercise regime is making time to exercise and not setting impossible goals. If you try and exercise every day, then that's great but you may find you flag and lose interest.

Choose something you enjoy doing and set times of the week when you will exercise for thirty minutes to an hour. A routine based on exercise every other day and weekends off may work for you. At the very least you will start to feel better, and, as you get fitter you will be able to exercise more and start losing weight (if that's your goal). You can increase the time you spend exercising as you get fitter but start with something realistic and which fits into your schedule.

If it is impossible to set a routine, then look at an exercise that can be enjoyed ad-hoc. I try and use my bicycle as much as I can for shopping or relaxation, I do this whenever the weather is good, and I have time. This cuts down the use of my car which is kinder to the environment, better for my pocket and good for my health.

During the winter you might find it more convenient to join a gym. I recently discovered a gym based in a local community centre. It has all the facilities the mainstream gyms have and has left me with no excuse for not exercising due to bad weather. Best of all it is, local and affordable.

SHELVE Tip

If you do not do any physical exercise, start thinking about which sports or exercises you may enjoy. If you can't think of any, then start by setting a time to start going for a ten-minute walk every other day. Review how you feel after a week. Do you feel better about exercising?

Use the space below to record your thoughts.

Diet

*"Pasta doesn't make you fat. How much pasta you eat
makes you fat"*

Giada De Laurentiis

Alongside exercise, a healthy diet, is another key factor in achieving good health.

I don't believe any particular diet is the answer to losing weight. Neither do I believe we should starve ourselves or deprive ourselves of enjoying the foods we love. It's more a question of eating in moderation.

A general rule with food is Brown is Good, White is Bad. So brown bread is healthier than white bread, brown rice or pasta healthier than white. It is the fibre in brown foods which make them healthier alternatives to their white counterparts. Fibre is better for our digestive system and these types of foods typically contain less sugar.

Anything with lots of sugar is bad so chocolate, and sugary drinks fall foul.

Most of us know this already and it's not rocket science, the more we eat of what's bad for us, and we most likely enjoy, the fatter we will become and as a result run the risk of increased health problems.

The problem with fad diets is most cut out one thing or another and this can be dangerous. If you look at diets online nearly all contradict each other. What one diet says is good for you the other will say is bad for you. Worryingly some will lack certain proteins or fats our bodies need to function properly.

So, what's the answer?

The answer is surprisingly simple. It is…. To eat a balanced and healthy diet crammed with the healthy things you love but treat yourself once a week with your favourite meal. Find the foods which work for you and you know to be healthy.

One of the reasons why a lot of French people enjoy good health is they eat what they want but very small amounts of the foods which can be fattening, in this way they keep trim and do not miss out on their favourite meals.

The following list contains suggestions you may want to include in your diet:

Vegetables – an obvious choice but find some you like and will enjoy eating. I find butter and a pinch of salt and pepper massively improves their flavour– especially cauliflower and broccoli. In the past, I never bothered with them much but now eat them at least once a week accompanied by a tin of tuna.

The good thing about vegetables is you can eat as much as you want.

Eggs – in moderation, they make a great start to the day and are a superfood. There is a nice slow ritual involved in whichever way you choose to cook and prepare them.

Salads, provided you don't smother them in mayonnaise and fattening dressings, you can eat more or less as much as you want. Rather than use a commercially prepared dressing try making your own with a small amount of Extra Virgin Olive Oil and some lemon juice. You can add further taste with a drizzle of Chili Oil and some fresh Coriander. Try and limit or avoid Mayonnaise as it is full of calories.

The key to a good dressing, like everything else, is to use good quality ingredients. A good quality Greek olive oil will be much tastier than a cheaper alternative. You can make salads more interesting by topping with crunchy onion sprinkles and some nuts (toasted or plain) sesame seeds are also a great healthy option.

If you find it hard to stick to a diet because you usually buy lunch out of convenience when you are working, then try taking your lunch with you. A very quick way of preparing lunch is to make your own Protein Smoothie in the morning and take it to work with some fresh fruit for lunch.

Buying a Smoothie Maker and making your own smoothies, containing a variety of fruits and vegetables, could transform your lunchtime ritual, as well as giving you a massive energy boost.

Simple, Slow and Vintage Living could act as good inspiration for your own Healthy Diet.

Pre 1970s very little food was processed or frozen. Most food was prepared fresh, and people were largely healthier and weighed less.

Take time to enjoy the ritual of cooking meals from scratch with healthy ingredients. A nice way of easing yourself into a healthier living lifestyle is to bring your friends along with you on the diet. Why not have friends over for dinner and cook something healthy, you can then take it in turns and share the experience? Hygge and Lagom are all about creating atmosphere, sharing experiences and moderation so incorporating these practices into a Diet will add an element of fun and make you more likely to succeed.

Think about how happy you are with your diet; do you need to lose weight? are you eating healthily? Is there anything you could do to improve your diet? Use the space below to record your thoughts.

Mental Exercise

"I believe depression is legitimate. But I also believe that if you don't exercise, eat nutritious food, get sunlight, get enough sleep, consume positive material, surround yourself with support, then you aren't giving yourself a fighting chance. "

Jim Carrey

Just as important as Physical Exercise is Mental Exercise. Our minds need challenging and exercising to stay alert. Mental exercise has been proven to help in staving off Alzheimer's and Dementia. There are many older people I know whose minds are very active and because of this, they remain healthy with a huge thirst for life.

Good ways to keep your mind active and working are to take up new hobbies, which require you to learn new skills, play games or challenge and tax your mind.

My belief is everyone should have at least two or three hobbies. The great thing about hobbies is it is never too late to start one and do something you have always wanted to do.

Below are some additional suggestions to help you keep your mind active:

* Dancing – learning a new dance routine, even if you can't dance, helps keep your mind agile and improves memory. It is the interaction of physical and mental activity which makes it a fun exercise
* Show or teach someone else your hobbies. Teaching others is a good way of reinforcing what you already know, and you may find yourself mentally challenged responding to questions
* Switch off your TomTom and use a map to find your way to a destination
* Learn a new Language
* Meditation, is a wonderful way to slow your mind and body down, reset and recharge.
* Keep a Journal, recording your thoughts is useful to look back on at a later date and is a way of measuring your progress. Writing and using an extended vocabulary is a great way to subconsciously exercise your mind.

SHELVE Tip

If you have never bothered with crosswords, then try completing a newspaper crossword – if you need to refer to other sources for the answers then treat that as part of the exercise. What matters is finding the answers and completing the crossword. How does it feel to complete a crossword?
Use the space below to record your thoughts.

The News

"He who laughs has not yet heard the bad news."

Bertolt Brecht

More and more people are switching off from the constant barrage of Mainstream Media News. I spent seven years working for a TV news station in their IT department. We covered a 24 x 7 shift rota. Mounted high up on the wall of our office was a speaker which constantly delivered the news. This could be a car crash killing ten people or a political event. Whatever the news announcement, it was never good. I would say less than 5% was good and very infrequently would it be uplifting.

This was at the start of 24-hour news coverage in the UK. The news programs would mainly repeat themselves during the day. Little has changed since then; in fact, it has gotten worse. We now have YouTube channels reporting the news based on hearsay from social media. The stories are presented in such a way that they give the impression of being corroborated, researched and investigated.

Quite often stories are speculation of what could or may happen. When it hasn't happened, it is forgotten about. The downside is that someone somewhere will have spent hours worrying about what could or could not happen. A recent example of this has been the massive meteor shower from the Sun that could have hit the earth – nothing happened but it got people worried unnecessarily. Another from a few years ago was the millennium bug, where we were led to believe planes would drop out of the sky, banking would crash and there would be general pandemonium all over the world once we were a second into the Year 2000.

We can debate the news and worry over it, or we can choose to limit our exposure to it. Thirty years ago, we didn't have rolling news and instead listened to an hourly update on the radio or waited till evening to watch the news on television.

By limiting our exposure to the news, we are clearing our minds of distractions, allowing us to concentrate on what's important, rather than worrying about things over which we have no control.

If you manage to miss the news for a couple of days, you won't have missed much and not much will have changed. Either whoever was being hounded to resign has resigned or the episode has blown over.

Ongoing stories will change but in the main not dramatically. So, you will have saved yourself two days of worrying about something you can do nothing about and will have had fun doing something you enjoy.

If you are a news addict, try setting a time of the day to watch or listen to the news rather than listening all day. After a few days think about how you feel? Do you still feel you need to listen all the time or are you feeling less anxious? If you are still feeling anxious, what else do you think you can do to limit your exposure, or do you find you enjoy the news?

If you need to keep up to date with the News for your work, is there a way you can limit the content to items that are relevant and filter out all the news you don't need?

Use the space below to record your thoughts.

Alcohol and Drinking

It is the wine that leads me on, the wild wine that sets the wisest man to sing at the top of his lungs, laugh like a fool — it drives the man to dancing... it even tempts him to blurt out stories better never told."

Homer, The Odyssey

We all know too much alcohol is bad for our health and our bank balances. But when do we start to know we need to do something about it and what do we do?

Most people start to recognise they have a problem when they realise they are spending too much time reading up on the ill effects of alcohol, wake up constantly feeling tired or call in sick to their workplace, one too many times.

We are all different and whilst some of us will wake up with hangovers, others will wake up as if they had drunk water all night.

Common signs of drinking too much are:

The need for a drink after work – this is the reward drink
Setting a time for that first drink – another reward drink
Fooling yourself into believing you have drunk less than you thought
Secretly procuring and disposing of the evidence
Not being able to stop at one or two drinks and feeling the need to finish the bottle
The belief red wine is good for you. Yes, a glass a day maybe but a bottle cancels out any benefit from moderate drinking and will cause long term problems
The belief white wine is good for you – as above
The belief rose wine is good for you – as above

Alcohol promises to make us feel good, yet in a lot of cases, it only serves to heighten any emotions we are going through. And that's not good if you're going through a particularly rough patch in your life.

Even if you are not going through a rough patch, the regular consumption of alcohol, in quantity, will start to cloud your judgement, sap your energy and affect your looks.

Everyone is aware of the calories in alcohol. It is fattening. Hours spent jogging or going to the gym can be wasted trying to get rid of nonproductive calories. The average bottle of wine contains 600 calories, so that's about 18,000 calories a month or 70 Big Macs if you have a bottle a day. Did you know a bottle of wine is the equivalent to two Big Macs?

Another major downside of alcohol is it affects your sleep. Some people swear blind they need a nightcap to fall asleep, however, alcohol does not induce the deep sleep our bodies need to be healthy. Sleep patterns are disturbed during the night with the need to visit the bathroom. All of this adds up to a bad night's sleep and is why people feel tired and lethargic after a night's heavy drinking.

The economic cost of drinking is high – say an inexpensive bottle of wine costs £5, and you consume a bottle a day – that's a massive £1,825 a year on an evening tipple. The cost of a couple of holiday breaks, or a PCP on a small car. Imagine the saving on a £10+ bottle of wine!

Social conditioning and subliminal messaging can play a large part in why people feel they need to drink.

Social Media is awash with images of champagne playing centre stage to a successful lifestyle. TV programmes and films regularly feature detectives hiding bottles of whisky in desk draws. In vintage films, it's not uncommon for drinking to feature, during the day, at a meeting, in the evening, in fact almost any occasion requiring celebration or consolation. It is not surprising therefore that it can feature prominently in our lives as we have been fed positive images of alcohol since childhood.

Finding happiness, wellbeing and living a simple more meaningful life is about being yourself, finding pleasure in the simple things in life, being healthy, being independent and being free from worries such as money.

If you are serious about turning around your life and achieving your goals, then there is no doubt an alcohol addiction will have an impact on how successful you are.

The first step is to recognise you may have a problem and you need to do something about it. If your addiction is serious then you should speak to your doctor or seek help from a local AA group.

Of course, most people do not have a problem with alcohol and can keep consumption under control whilst still enjoying a drink now and again.

If you feel your alcohol consumption is something you are uncomfortable with, but it is still allowing you to carry on with your life then the tips below may help.

- Try having a break from alcohol two or more evenings a week or only drinking every other night

- Do not keep more alcohol in your home than you need for one evening – try buying smaller bottles of spirits or wine for one evening. It is much cheaper and stops you from overindulging. Be aware that starting with small bottles may lead you to buy bigger bottles after a while as it's more cost-effective and you are then back on the treadmill

- Keep a weekly diary of how much you are consuming – this can be a real wakeup call

- Recognise your triggers - at the time you would normally have your first drink, or in a situation where you feel compelled to have a drink - do something else instead – go for a walk or a run, anything that gets you past the need for a drink

- Instead of wine as your evening treat, Buy something else like cookies or alcohol-free wine

There are dangers in just going cold turkey, if you have set your goal too high you may find you fall off the wagon too often and end up binge drinking, which can be much worst.

What worked for me was to swap out regular dinks for their low alcohol alternatives. Usually, these are 0.5% and taste pretty good and are of course much cheaper.

You still get the feeling of being a grown-up and having a glass of wine but without the hangover. Eventually, I got to the stage where I preferred the taste of low alcohol wine to full strength wine. There are so many different varieties of alcohol-free wine, using the same grapes as regular wine. Most supermarkets now stock one of their own together with a mainstream brand. If they are hard to find it's because they are usually tucked away on the bottom shelf.

Alcohol-Free wine gives you all the associated health benefits of full-strength wine but without the calorific content. That's because the calories in wine are derived from the sugar used to produce the alcoholic content.

Low alcohol drinks are now available in most pubs and bars so you can enjoy socialising over a drink without getting drunk. Because the alcoholic content is almost zero you may find the cravings start to go and it becomes a nice drink to have whilst making dinner, relaxing at the end of the day or when socialising.

If you enjoy a daily drink, try swapping some days for low alcohol days and then increase these days so it becomes the norm rather than the exception. The goal should be to replace the low alcohol drink when you feel ready with a non-alcoholic drink, such as water, tea, or coffee etc.

Cutting down or quitting alcohol is a great time to set physical goals such as losing weight. You will see the fruits of your efforts much quicker. This in turn will provide you with motivation to carry on and start setting more ambitious goals.

There are plenty of resources on the internet and help available if you are concerned about your drinking. Don't be scared to seek advice, it is better to seek advice today than wait for tomorrow.

Keep a record of the amount of alcohol you have consumed over a week and record this in the space below and the next page. Do you think this is too much or about right? Are you happy with the amount of alcohol you are drinking?
Record a week's worth of alcohol consumption in the space below if you wish.

Smoking and Vaping

"You are greater than your addiction"

Nasia Davos

Smoking, vaping and alcohol dependency are in my opinion pretty much the same thing, with the exception drinking is more likely to trigger the need for a cigarette than a cigarette triggers the need for a drink.

Both smoking and drinking are bad for your health, pocket, and wellbeing. Most of the previous chapter on alcohol can be applied to this chapter, however, there are some differences.

The downside of smoking is:

It is bad for your health and linked to all sorts of cancers
Eventually it hampers the enjoyment of physical activities which are good for us
It is bad for your finances. A pack a day at £10 is the equivalent of £3650 a year
The smell of smoke gets in your clothes, hair, and home. You may not notice it, but other people will
You feel like a social outcast having to leave a meal to have a cigarette
Unless you smoke outside, your home will smell of smoke
Even if you do smoke outside then the smell will waft in after you

So, what can you do about it?

There are several options open to you, one of which is to make a conscious decision to just give up. There are many well-known tried and tested ways of giving up: nicotine gum, tablets, hypnotherapy etc.

I tried a lot of different methods to give up smoking: hypnosis, patches, chewing gum etc. What worked in the end for me, was to introduce vaping. This enabled me to gradually come off cigarettes and use my Vape with nicotine in it. I gradually smoked fewer and fewer cigarettes as I switched to vaping. Once I had quit cigarettes, I then reduced the nicotine in the Vape to zero and then quit vaping a couple of years later.

The advantage of switching from cigarettes to vaping, if you are unable to give up under the normal methods is, according to many sources, that it is less harmful than smoking real cigarettes. Your need for a cigarette is met with the Vape device and you start to feel much healthier in a short space of time.

Activities such as cycling and running become easier and of course, that horrible cough has gone along with the smell of smoke. After a while you'll find whenever you get a whiff of someone else's smoke you'll wonder why you ever smoked in the first place.

Of course, giving up a habit such as smoking is difficult, some say near impossible, while switching to a Vape device there will be times when you crave a normal cigarette, and you will have one.

The best thing is to not beat yourself up over it, once you have been vaping for a while, smoking a cigarette will taste terrible and you won't be tempted to smoke another.

There are no set time scales for how quickly you can give up, it varies from person to person, what is important is that you stick with it.

Perseverance is key, one or two relapses doesn't mean you have to give up on vaping or that it isn't working. Every time you use the Vape it is one less cigarette smoked.

Try and keep a spare Vape in your car or your bag, that way if something does go wrong, you don't have an excuse to buy cigarettes. Persevere and you will switch from smoking to vaping.

The next stage, in time, is to quit vaping. I got fed up having to make sure I had enough liquid and the constant replacing of batteries and coils which kept failing.

Quitting vaping I found to be strange as it's not the nicotine you are missing but simply the act of vaping. You may start to realise that you have been vaping more often than you were having a cigarette. I found myself pretending to vape on a pen for a few days when I stopped vaping.
In retrospect and ideally, it would be better to switch directly from smoking to vaping, reduce nicotine to zero and quit vaping in a much shorter timeframe. However not everyone can do this, and I certainly couldn't have quit permanently had I tried to rush the process.

So, the advantages are clear and the biggest benefits you will see are in your health, your finances and in the way other people see you.

As with all life choices you should do your own research. Particularly into any dangers of vaping. You should also consult your GP to check that this course of action is suited to you.

If you are a Smoker, consider buying a disposable e-cigarette the next time you buy a packet of cigarettes. Try smoking it instead of every other cigarette and see if this helps make the pack last longer. If you are finding it easy then use the e-cigarette more. Save having a traditional cigarette until you need one. Hopefully, this will help you move from cigarettes to vaping.

If you are a Vaper, then try getting a blank or empty vapouriser and using that to inhale on instead of a loaded, working vapouriser. Try swapping out every other vape with the blank and increase. You will need to keep doing this for some time but eventually, you may find you no longer need the vapouriser.

Use the space below to record your thoughts or plans.

Economics

Economics is a vast area, we could be talking about Home Economics, Personal Finances or even the Economics of the country. Let's leave your country's Economics out of this discussion and concentrate on Personal Finances. Home Economics are natural elements of Simple, Slow and Vintage Living.

Many say "Money" is the route of all evil, but it is also the route to happiness. Without it, most of us would not be able to lead the lifestyles which make us happy and content.

You will read many blogs saying money doesn't matter, and you can be happy without it. But this simply isn't true, everybody needs a certain amount of money to have choices on how they live their life.

I've been without money in the past and I wasn't happy or content. The harder I worked the more I spent and the more I got into debt. I thought buying new things would make me happy, but after a couple of months, I grew bored of the item and was saddled with paying it off.

Putting a holiday on a credit card seems like a great way of getting away from it all but when you come back from holiday, all your problems are still there, and you have an extra debt to pay off.

Being short of money is expensive. You are forced into having to do things which by their very nature are poor value for money. You have to drive a car that is expensive to tax, uses more fuel and breaks down more often with costly repair bills.

Your service supplies like Gas and Electricity might be on a pay as you go meter, and these are much more expensive than the quarterly billing types.

You have little choice over energy supplies, credit card companies, loans, mortgages and where to shop. Money gives you these choices and allows you to make the decisions you want to make. For example, having a more economical and reliable car frees up money to spend on quality items such as food. Better quality food is healthier and tastier, so you feel better.

Being poor makes it harder to do your bit for the environment due to the limited choices you have over transport, heating and food.

That said, too much money can come with a whole new set of problems. How do I protect it? how much should I spend? what if I lose it? how can I get more?

"Too many people spend money they earned to buy things they don't want to impress people that they don't like."

Will Rogers

What we need is enough money to be comfortable so that we don't need to worry about the future. If you have too much money, then you are in a fortunate position and can look at ways of investing it.

For obvious reasons this book cannot give Financial Advice, but I can give you advice on how to start cutting back on expenses and saving money makes it easier to reduce debt and achieve your own goals.

As with most topics, there is plenty of advice out there and it is up to you how much advice you take.

Where to start

The best place to start is by honestly looking at your situation and working out where you stand. Without knowing where you are today you have no way of working out where you can be tomorrow.

Go through your bank statement and list every standing order and direct debit so you know what your outgoings are. Don't forget to include subscriptions such as streaming services, these may be paid for through PayPal, Apple Pay or other less obvious means. Then list all your debts on credit cards and loans. What you should have is a list like this:

Outgoings	Monthly Amount	Debt	Amount
Rent/ Mortgage	£750	Mortgage	£200,000
Gas/Electric	£90	Car Loan	£5,000
Insurance	£20	Credit Card	£2,000
Council Tax	£80		
Car Tax and Insurance	£40		
Car Loan	£160		
Credit Card Min Payment	£15		
Total	**£1,155**		**£207,000**

Then work out what your expenses are every week

Remember to include everything you spend money on, this will vary from week to week but try and get a rough average figure.

An example is:

Food to cook at home	£75
Takeaways	£30
Coffee	£15
Petrol/Fuel	£30
Entertainment	£70
Cigarettes	£70
Alcohol at home	£35
Total	£325

So, a monthly total would be roughly £325 x 52 (weeks in a year) divided by 12 (months) = £1408.33 Add to that your outgoings of £1,155 and you have a total of £2,563.33 going out every month.

Now add together all your incomings. In this example, it is £3,000 a month.

So that leaves £3,000 minus £2,563.33 = £436.67

Now you know how much you owe and how much you have left to start paying things off you are in a good place to start taking control of your finances rather than them controlling you.

Formulating a plan

If you are experiencing real financial problems, you should always speak to your lenders first and see if you can reach an agreement. There is no shame in being honest with them and they will be grateful you have been, it shows you are keen to be a good customer. If your income is less than your outgoings, then you must speak to your creditors as it means you are increasing your debt every month making it more and more difficult to make plans for reducing it.

The next step is to go through all your outgoings and see where you can reduce them. Here are some examples:

<u>Historical Insurance and Warranty Premiums which have auto-renewed</u>

All too easily we can have taken out insurance for something which is no longer needed. Electrical shops will always try and sell you product insurance. Sometimes you may find it worthwhile for peace of mind, however, bear in mind you should get a statutory 12-month warranty on an item as standard and if the manufacturer has confidence in a product, they will often give you an additional year's warranty on top of the statutory term. It is also worth checking with the manufacturer the terms of their extended warranty as this can work out cheaper than taking a retailer warranty out. In the past, I've been caught out by warranties that just didn't live up to the hype and didn't pay out. I once took out an extended warranty on a used car, when it came to claiming on it, I was blanked. But they remembered me when they wanted me to pay for another year! Always, do your research on the internet and find out what other people think of the insurance or warranty before signing on the dotted line.

How much TV do you watch and what do you watch? How much TV do we need? With so many TV subscription services available it is really easy to pay for services you don't need. Just over ten years ago my Sky+ satellite receiver packed up and I had just bought one of the first of the second-generation Apple TV boxes. As I didn't have a TV aerial, I couldn't receive terrestrial television, so all my viewing has been through the Sky+ box. What I found was, in the main, I watched Films and was beginning to watch more and more YouTube. So, I decided to not replace the Sky+ box and use Apple TV instead. This meant I was no longer watching any live TV and as a result, I was no longer subjected to adverts. I won't pretend it was easy to make the switch and it probably took a good six months or so before I stopped missing live TV. However, once I realised I could take control of what I was watching and when I could watch it, the better I felt and the more I felt like I was controlling the TV and not being a slave to it. It is surprising how much content is freely available. DVDs are now only a few pounds in thrift stores and YouTube contains a wealth of freely available films, shows and creative content by YouTubers. In addition, there are subscription services that will give you quite selective content depending on what you need. So don't be afraid to cut back, take control and save money.

Magazine and Music Streaming Service Subscriptions

In just the same way Insurance premiums can get out of control, so too can magazine and music subscriptions. It is now quite popular to pay for a subscription for a magazine to your tablet and then find out months later you're no longer reading it. Or the tablet breaks, you get a new one and don't install everything onto it.

Music subscriptions are only really worth it if you listen to a lot of new music all the time. If you are listening to the same music, then you are paying for the music many times over. It is said that after 19 plays of an album through a streaming service, it is more environmentally friendly to have either bought and downloaded the album or purchased it on a CD. Ask yourself if you get enough out of the streaming service to justify the cost. Remember, saving just £10 a month adds up to £120 a year. If you are subscribing to magazines and music, then you could be spending at least £240 a year on something you don't need.

<u>Phone contracts that exceed your needs</u>

Check your Mobile phone bill and make sure it meets your needs. Are you paying for unlimited calls and texts and only using a tiny amount; do you use an application like WhatsApp most of the time for calls and texts? Do you use your data allowance, or can you cut back? Finally, do you need to change your phone every time you are due a renewal or can you keep your phone for a couple of years longer or until it breaks? Most of the time, upgrades are just slight improvements on what you already have, maybe wait until there is a significant upgrade and then upgrade.

Whilst you are checking your Mobile Phone bill, don't forget to check your Landline/Internet bill. A very little publicised fact is you can now get Internet/Wi-Fi contracts without a contract for a landline. In the past, you used to have to pay for a landline, even if you never used it. At the time of writing being able to switch to an Internet-only service with an existing supplier isn't possible, however, you can switch if you take out a new contract with a new supplier.

<u>Paying a Gym Subscription and never going</u>

This is one of the most common ways of wasting money. At the start of the year many of us take out gym subscriptions on special offers, after a few months of good intentions we tell ourselves we will go at some point, yet we never do. If you want to lose weight and get fit then find something that fits in with your schedule.

It is surprising the number of things we pay for which we don't even use. I once unwittingly subscribed to an online shopping discount offer. I didn't realise I was paying for it until I noticed a £15 debit on my account every month. Once I worked out what it was, I cancelled the subscription, but it must have cost me about £250 for something I didn't even use.

<u>Entitlements and Allowances</u>

It is really easy to overlook any allowances you may be entitled to. For example, single person council tax allowance and your Tax Code.

<u>Check the Market</u>

Insurance and utility companies all rely on us being too lazy to shop around when it is time to renew their policy. It's good practice to shop around using Internet Comparison sites when you reach the end of a deal or contract. Quite often when you threaten to take your business elsewhere, suppliers will offer you a better deal to stay.

Getting Organised

A good tip is to have three bank accounts, one for your monthly bills, one for spending money and one for savings. This way you can easily keep a track of how much you must spend, where your money is going, and you can start to see the rewards of saving.

A common goal for most people is to start reducing debt to free up money making it easier to reduce other debt. Start with the debts having the highest interest rate or that are easy to clear quickly.

In the example above there is a credit card debt of £2000 but only a minimum payment of £15 a month. This debt is going to take forever to clear and attracts a high-interest rate, but it has a low payment. However, with £436 left a month, £250 could go towards clearing the £2000 debt and it would be gone in eight months.

Another approach may be to look at where else money is going and free up some to clear the debt. Giving up smoking and drinking at home frees up £105 a week, that's £455 a month which with the £250 is enough to clear the debt in about 10 weeks. The car could then be cleared during the rest of that first year and in the second year our example would be better off annually by:

Monthly Car Payments	£1,920
Drinking at home	£1,820
Smoking	£3,640
Total Saving	**£7,380**

So, the revised amount of non-allocated income is the original £436, plus the (£7,380 divided by 12 months) £615 a month from the savings above giving £1,051 monthly – enough to start looking at clearing the mortgage, topping up pensions or savings, in fact, anything you set as a goal.

Of course, not everyone smokes, and drinks and situations vary. Changes do not happen overnight, they take time. The example above is meant as an illustration. You may, for example, want to carry on drinking at home and save the money by ditching the Frappuccino on the way into the office.

The importance of saving a little every month

"Do not save what is left after spending but spend what is left after saving."

Warren Buffett

Rather than thinking about how much cash you have leftover to save, why not budget for saving and what's left over is for spending? No matter how much cash you earn, it is really important to save a little so you build up a safety net. By building a safety net you are catering for unexpected expenses such as a boiler or car breakdown.

The psychological benefits of saving are enormous in that the worry of being able to deal with an unexpected expense is much reduced, and you start building your self-esteem. This is because if something does happen you don't need to ask a friend or relative for help. For me, it started when I was younger, and I decided to get a dog - the sheer worry of unexpected Vet bills was enormous. Saving alleviated those concerns and meant I could enjoy spending time with my dog rather than worry about her getting ill. If you find you need to dip into your safety net, it doesn't matter, that's what it's there for.

Looking after the pennies – want or need?

Now you have a plan, here are some practical tips to help you start controlling your spending.

There is an old saying "Look after the pennies and the pounds will look after themselves" This is still true today. Many people will buy a coffee on the way to work, adding this daily expense up over a month can add up to between £40 and £50. A cheaper alternative is to buy a reusable mug and make your own before leaving home.

Online shopping has become more and more a part of our daily lives, you think of something you want and within a minute you can order it online, then it's forgotten about. But do you need it or is it just something you want? The things we want outweigh the things we need and this is where we can needlessly waste money.

Rather than ordering spontaneously why not compile a list of things you need and order these in one go at the start of the month or when you have just been paid? The total cost will question whether these things are necessities or nice to have. It also cuts down the number of deliveries to your home and with that the cost in carbon emissions.

Think twice buy once

How many times have you bought something on the spur of the moment? It is something we have all done and then lived to regret.

A good rule to follow is to think twice and buy once. If you are unsure on whether or not to buy something, particularly if it is expensive, walk away, have a think and then go back and buy the item if It is what you really want.

The four basic rules to buying anything are:

Can I afford it
Do I need it?
Do I love it?
Will it last?

Of primary consideration is the cost of the item, can you afford to buy it without getting into debt?

Things like cars and houses are items most people have a loan of some kind for, but if you are buying something like a watch, is it worth getting into debt for a Nice-to-have a piece of jewellery? If you can easily afford it then there isn't a problem, but if you can't then you need to question whether or not it is a necessity.

If you have set a monthly budget and your savings goal, look at the impact the purchase will have on those goals and then look again as to whether it is a wise decision. If you are replacing an item that is still working, ask yourself if it can last longer until you can comfortably afford to buy what you really want.

Do I love it? – by that I mean does the item please you, is it aesthetically pleasing, will it give you pleasure using it or will it get thrown in a drawer or end up at the thrift store after a couple of months?

Will it last? – is it good enough quality to last? It is pointless and wasteful to buy something because it is cheap and if it isn't good quality in the first place, it won't last. There are too many examples of cheap electronic devices failing after their warranty period only to end up in landfills. This is not only costly to the individual in terms of having to constantly buy replacements, but it is incredibly harmful to the environment.

Taking control of your money, spending and planning for a simple, financially independent life is key to finding happiness, wellbeing and realising your long-term life goals.

Start a new spreadsheet and record all your outgoing into one sheet, together with the dates that any Direct Debits or Standing Orders are taken. When you have your spreadsheet, ask yourself if you are happy with the amount you are saving? Are there any savings you could make? Do you have a target for saving? Record your thoughts in the space below.

Social

Emotional Baggage

"You cannot move on to a new phase in life if you bring your old baggage with you, let the bad go, and move onto the new"

Patrick Read Johnson

To move forward we need to clear the decks and unfortunately part of this means breaking off relationships that are not productive or good for our well-being.

Too many people stay in relationships that are toxic because they are frightened to break away from them or fear they will offend someone.

This is where the importance of financial security comes back into play. Far too often people stay in a relationship because without that relationship they become financially unstable.

The word NO is incredibly powerful and a great way of relieving stress. By simply saying No you don't want to do something, you will feel empowered and the stress building up in advance of the event will be lost.

Far too often we do things we don't want to do, and we do these things out of obligation.

Of course, there are times when saying No is not an option, it may be a work meeting, or you have to work with someone you don't like very much. By seeking financial independence, you give yourself the option of saying No in the longer term and seeking another position or doing something else.

No one should be afraid of just being truthful and saying No to something. After a while, it becomes easier and the time freed up from doing something you don't really want to do gives you time to do something you really want to do, which is far more productive and enjoyable.

Some of the most powerful and successful people in the world are where they are because they have learnt to say No to things that are not productive and yes to things they believe are.

When something stops being enjoyable it is no longer adding to your sense of wellbeing, and it is not a productive activity.

A good place to start is to look at which activities and people you deal with daily. On a sheet of paper record on one side people and activities you enjoy and on the other side those people and activities you do not enjoy.

Plan to cease the activities you do not enjoy and to stop seeing the people who do not contribute to your wellbeing.

Simply cutting down email/social media consumption will help distance yourself from people or activities you find toxic or non-productive.

By cutting down or out the activities and people we do not like, we can concentrate and devote more attention to worthwhile activities and relationships.

In an ideal world, everyone would just be doing what they wanted and seeing who they wanted to see, but life isn't like that, however, we each have it in our power to change and to take control and say No to affect long term changes and gain control of our lives.

SHELVE Tip

Think of something you have to do, that you would rather not do. Is the task important? What impact will not doing it have on you? Can you say NO the next time you are asked to do it? Try and say NO to at least one thing and see how you feel.

Use the space below to record your thoughts.

Difficult People and Bullying

"Courage is fire, and bullying is smoke"

Benjamin Disraeli

Sometimes it is not going to be possible to say no, particularly if it is to your boss at work. Work is the place in which we are most likely to meet difficult people. These are unfortunately people we are forced to work with but which we would not normally have associated ourselves within our normal social sphere.

I've had this happen to me and I'm sure nearly everyone reading this book will have had it happen.

The best way I have found to deal with difficult people at work, is to have a three-pronged approach.

Firstly, try and find out more about the person and why they are being difficult. You can do this by asking them for examples of what they think you should be doing, or, how they would approach a task they have criticised you for.

In a work situation the reasons why people are difficult may be:

- They are unsure of their abilities
- They are threatened by you
- They feel that by being seen as a "hard person" they will get recognition and promotion
- They have been bullied themselves in the past

Secondly, once you know why they are being difficult, try and work out a way forward and a way in which you can mutually respect each other.

Questions such as "how can we work together on this?" or "how can I help?" or "can you help me?"

What this effectively means is you are levelling up. For example, a bully will see themselves as having the upper hand or being the bigger person. By eliminating any feelings of being less superior to the bully from your mind, you become equal and therefore the bully has nothing to intimidate you with. Try doing this by saying hello in a bold manner to whoever it is that is being difficult or asking them straightforward questions.

Don't be afraid to challenge someone being difficult with you.

If this stage doesn't work, then it is time to move to stage 3.

The Third stage is acceptance. By acceptance I mean that either you work out a way to work together or you decide you cannot work with this person and escalate the matter to a more senior manager. Be careful with this approach as too many escalations and you will be seen as the problem.

In accepting a situation, you should visualise yourself as having risen above the situation. You are in control and the person causing you grief is a temporary irritation. You have tried to level up and this hasn't worked, so now, you will be the one who will remain calm and distant, because at the end of the day you have other plans for your future.

It is mentally much easier to accept you will not agree with everyone and everyone has different thoughts. You do not have to agree with them, but you do not have to challenge them if it is going to cause you upset.

Life simply isn't worth it. It is much better to work on another goal to distance yourself from that person or situation than it is to waste time engaging in a conflict that serves no productive outcome for yourself.

The other problem in remaining engaged in a non-productive relationship is it becomes exhausting, and with exhaustion comes fatigue and when you are fatigued you lose motivation in other areas of your life. It may not be obvious at first. Usually, it will take the form of annoyance with the other person, eventually, this becomes subconsciously exhausting, mentally draining and will sap your energy. At worst it will act as a blocker to you achieving your goals.

My own example of this was when I was employed in a role dealing with problems in an extremely unhappy customer base. I would come home at the end of the day exhausted and upset. I tried hard to resolve the problems but no matter what I did, the problems were outside my control.

When I realised the people I was meeting with during the day were not annoyed with me but with my organisation, I was able to start visualising what they were thinking and what they were going through. So, I developed empathy with them, and this made it easier to communicate the problems back to my organisation. Even though my organisation could not efficiently deal with the problems, I felt better that I understood the customer and had played my part in communicating their issues back to my organisation.

Now whilst this provided a temporary relief there were still people that I didn't get on with. Some of them I was able to work with by distancing myself, viewing the interactions as purely objective in achieving a common goal. The people that I couldn't gain any commonality with I further distanced and just remained objective. I chose to switch off when I finished work and concentrate instead on a recreational hobby.

Distancing and separating my work life from my personal life helped enormously. Predictably the role came to a natural end, and I was able to move on.

Life is full of change and not liking something right now is not the end of the world as it is bound to change.

SHELVE Tip

Are you being harassed or bullied by someone in your life? Try and think of a strategy for dealing with that person the next time you see them. If you don't feel that's going to work, then try and speak to someone about it. Write down your strategy and thoughts in the space below as there may be other strategies that come to mind when you have finished reading this book.

Social Media

"You learn the hard way. That's the thing with social media. Nobody knows what they're doing."

Cameron Dallas

If we are engaged in social media then we have to accept that sometimes things may not always be positive and as a result, our wellbeing and happiness will be affected. There have been many stories of teenagers suffering from depression and anxiety as a direct result of posts on social media. Bullying can be indirect and commonplace whether intentional or not.

Social Media, when used correctly, can be a great source of entertainment, but used incorrectly it can be destructive and leave us with feelings of inadequacy.

There are obvious Social Media platforms such as Facebook, Instagram, and Twitter. The less obvious platforms are Television, Radio, WhatsApp, and Magazines. All of these have one thing in common. They try to show or influence us in how to live our lives. They do this through images and stories of people they think we should aspire to be.

There is a need in society to be seen to be doing well. The reality is in "keeping up with the Jones's" today we are depriving ourselves of the futures which will make us happy tomorrow. If we are constantly seeking the next best thing then we will never enjoy what we have now.

The word "Luxury" has never been so overused as it is now. TV Programmes and social media is awash with people leading Luxury lifestyles, driving Luxury cars, and wearing designer Luxury clothes. All of this is of course possible and achievable if you prioritise spending your money on these items. If you can't afford to buy them outright, then you can have them through a subscription-based service or purchase on credit. The problem is they are not owned by you, and someone somewhere is making money out of your desires.

Controlling your Social Media engagement is no different to any other form of decluttering. If we look at Facebook, for example, an approach might be:

- Decide what it is you are getting out of Facebook, why are you using it, who do you want to keep in contact with? Unfriend people you no longer want to keep in contact with or do not bring anything positive to your life

- Decide which groups you want to be involved with, which groups make you feel positive and which groups annoy or irritate you. Leave the groups which are not bringing anything meaningful to your life

- Look for groups aligning with your interests as a way of replacing the groups of people you are no longer interested in

- Limit your time looking at Facebook, cut back slowly at first before eventually leading to checking in two or three times a week

- Remove the Facebook app from your phone if it is installed and just use it on your computer

- Think twice before posting on social media. Is what you are saying accurate, will it cause harm, are you happy for the world to read what you have said?

There is a wealth of information on the internet and discussion groups around Simple, Slow and Vintage Living. Controlling social media so you get what you want out of it opens a massive resource pool to learn from other people and engage in conversation about topics that are of interest to you.

SHELVE Tip

Look at your social media accounts and see how many people you have listed and ask yourself if they are people you know and your friends or can you unfriend or remove them. Are they adding anything to your life? Do you benefit from having them as a friend on your social media account or could your time be better spent reading pages that are of interest to you?

Use the space below to record your thoughts.

Relationship Breakups

"We must be willing to let go of the life we've planned, to have the life that is waiting for us."

Joseph Campbell

It is a sad and true fact of life that nearly all of us at some point or another in our lives will go through a relationship breakup. Sometimes it is mutual, sometimes not, sometimes planned and sometimes not.

With a breakup comes extremes of emotions regardless of who initiated the breakup. If you break up with someone you either feel guilty or relieved. If you are the one being broken up with then you can feel rejection, hurt, anger or possibly relief.

There are no obvious answers on how to recover from a breakup and everyone deals with this particular life event in their way. Sometimes we get over it quickly, for example, if we saw it coming or we were not that bothered about the person. And at other times we take it very personally and it takes a long time to get over the relationship.

Someone once said to me that for every year you are with someone it takes half a year to get over them. That's quite a long time and in general, I would say that if it is a deep relationship then it takes that length of time to get to the stage where you are coming to terms with the breakup and able to move on.

Are there any magic answers or shortcuts? Unfortunately not, but some tips can help make your recovery easier:

*   It's not your fault. Don't spend time thinking about who did or said what to who – it's too late and won't achieve anything.

- You are not the only person to have gone through this. Breakups happen every hour of every day of every year to someone in the world. You're not the first and not the last.

- You will get over it. No matter how bad it feels you will get over it, people always do. The younger and more inexperienced at relationships you are the worse it is.

- Talk to someone. By talking to someone you are helping to get your feelings out. Listen to what you are saying and imagine you are the person listening, what advice would you give?

- Don't turn to alcohol. This will only make things worse – do something else instead like listening to music. There are millions of feel-good songs out there which will help you get over a breakup and one day in the future, when you hear that song again it will bring back happy memories rather than bad ones.

- Replace the relationship with something constructive, look at what new hobbies you could take on. Maybe you could study for something or learn a new skill or get super fit? Turn the failed relationship into a success story. "Because of X, I managed to do Y"

When you start on a journey to improve life because you want to improve it, you will find you start looking at the positives in a situation. Whatever happens, can be turned into a positive. It doesn't matter what it is, as one door closes, another opens and so it is with the end of a relationship. It just means it wasn't right, and something better is around the corner. The "something better" could be anything, it could be another person, your career, anything. Life is full of opportunities, and it is up to you what you make of them.

For me, the Madonna song "Power of Goodbye" says everything that needs to be said about the end of a relationship. The song is about empowerment and moving on better and stronger. The evolving you has been made possible by the fact that you've had the relationship. Music can be both powerful and a great healer.

And remember that eventually, once the hurt has passed, you may one day look back on the relationship with fondness. We can't change the past, but we can learn from it and use those experiences to create fantastic futures.

SHELVE Tip

Take some time to reflect on your past relationships. How do you feel now that some time has passed? How would you have handled things differently and what have you learnt? Our lives are about learning from the past and the lessons learnt are learnt so that they help us with our futures. We should never regret anything, we should just learn.

Use the space below to record your thoughts.

Finding and Making New Friends

"You can't stay in your corner of the Forest waiting for others to come to you. You have to go to them sometimes."

A.A. Milne, Winnie-the-Pooh

When we are young it is easy to find and make new friends, as we get older it becomes more difficult. Partly because we become more rooted in our ways and partly because everyone around us has grown older and they too are becoming routed in their ways. Sometimes it is because the people around us are preoccupied with families and their existing circle of friends.

So how do we make new friends? Unsurprisingly there are hundreds of ways of making new friends but let's list just six of them

- Start a new hobby which involves meeting people – sports are a good example

- See if there are any social activities at work you could join in

- Look at local events and see if there are any activities you are interested in

- Go for a walk, be friendly – say hello to people if they look at you

- Look online, there are many forums and special interest websites with online communities

- Remember the secret is to look for people doing something you enjoy or are interested in. If you have something in common, then you are halfway there.

Two major considerations worth bearing in mind when making new friends are if you meet a large group of people, don't necessarily make friends straight away with the friendliest person. All too often these turn out to be the people you don't get on with and the most difficult to get to know are the ones that are your friends.

Take your time, you don't need a friend straight away. Secondly don't spend too much time trying to re-kindle old friendships, if they have petered out then there is a reason why. Sometimes it can be successful but all too often we realise why we lost contact in the first place.

SHELVE Tip

Are you happy with the number of friends you have, do you want more, or do you have too many? What can you do about the situation? Record your thoughts in the space below

Social Aspects of Hygge and Lagom

Hygge (The Danish Way to Live Well) and Lagom (The Swedish Art of Balanced Living) both have social elements to their lifestyle choices, they are good examples of SHELVE Fusion, both fall into the category of lifestyle choice but are also useful facilitators.

A fundamental part of Hygge is the getting together of people with their friends to enjoy being together in a nice safe, warm, cosy space. The getting together could be over dinner, sharing tea in front of a fire, coffee, TV or Games evenings etc. The most popular group size for Hygge is between three and four people, but people can practice Hygge on their own or groups of up to ten and beyond sometimes.

Popular in Sweden and part of Lagom is Fika, this is the regular getting together with work colleagues for a break during the day to drink coffee, eat something tasty and have a good chat.

There's a lot other countries can learn from Hygge and Lagom, beware though, socialising constantly within a small group can become insular and difficult for others outside the group to break in.

There's more on Hygge and Lagom in the next part of this book.

SHELVE Tip

After reading more on Hygge in this book why not plan a Hygge get together for a group of three or four friends? If you go ahead, why not write down who you will invite, when and any preparations you need to make in the space below.

Environment

"One of the first conditions of happiness is that the link between man and nature shall not be broken"

Leo Tolstoy

No one can have escaped the Climate Crisis. In the same way, regular news can cause unnecessary worry, so too can the threat of the imminent destruction of the world, and the need to change our lives dramatically if we are to avoid Armageddon.

We can of course all play our part, and I do as much as I can so I feel confident I have achieved all I can as an individual. There are some things, however, I cannot change as they are simply not practical, affordable, or doable at this stage and I feel that's ok. We all need to feel comfortable we are all doing as much as we can and playing our part.

By adopting a Simple, Slow and Vintage Life, you are naturally steering yourself towards a more sustainable way of living.

Unfortunately, if you are looking at a slower simpler way of life and live in the countryside or a small village you will probably need a car. This is especially true if you are seeking out locally sourced produce, secondhand items of furniture etc. Don't feel guilty about having a car, just use it responsibly and if you can, cycle or walk instead. Plan trips for shopping so you are visiting multiple shops in a day rather than separately, it will cut down on your expenses and cut down on emissions.

It is disappointing that with all the talk of global warming and, previous to that, natural fuels running out, we build ever bigger cars. Cars over the past few years have grown larger and larger, in part I suppose to meet safety legislation. But how much better would it be if there was a limit as to how large a car could be and how large an engine it could have? Of course, with Petrol and Diesel cars being phased out this becomes academic, other than no doubt cars will continue to grow and become more complex.

The Vintage/Simple/Slow living person in me says that in the future we should try and migrate existing cars from fossil fuel to electric whilst a Lagom voice is telling me that the cars should be just the right size, not too big and not too small.

I try and buy as much stuff as I can from independent local retailers. To me, this is much better than buying from big supermarkets as the local produce has not had to travel hundreds of miles in lorries and in some cases across Europe.

Shopping locally gives local businesses a chance to develop and thrive, it helps local people create their own sustainable economy and takes money away from the large corporates and puts it into the hands of ordinary people.

Take a moment to consider the number of lorries on the road. In recent years this has risen considerably, in part this is due to a large number of supermarkets there are in the country and the ever-increasing demand for more variety in the products they offer.

In the past a shop would have had one type of Baked Beans, now all four local supermarkets will stock that same brand together with other brands and their own. This means there are now four or five times as many lorries delivering Baked Beans than there would have been in the past. Whilst there's not much we can do to change how other people shop, we can take responsibility for how we shop, as individuals, and make choices that give us the knowledge, we are limiting our effect on globalisation as much as we can.

If you have the space to grow vegetables and keep livestock then you are one of the few fortunate people who can accelerate a path towards your happiness and wellbeing by living a more independent sustainable lifestyle that truly embraces simple, slow, and vintage living.

Before Supermarkets, it was common for households to grow their own vegetables. If we can start doing this again then we reduce our reliance on products which have been sprayed with insecticides, wrapped in plastic, and then shipped by lorry across the country. An added benefit is they taste better too.

Another way of helping the environment, your health and your pocket are to stop buying ready meals and instead batch cook and freeze your own healthy meals. They will taste much better due to the better-quality ingredients, be healthier due to the control you have over salt, fat and sugar and it is kinder to the environment as you eliminate the need for packaging and transportation.

We are all aware of the need to reduce our electricity consumption and this is relatively straightforward, switch to low energy bulbs, turn off electronic devices when they are not in use rather than leaving them on standby and don't run washing machines and dishwashers half empty. If you can get an energy meter installed, then you monitor how much energy you are using and how much electricity certain devices use. It was said at one time a domestic home laser printer costs around £30 in electricity a year if it is left switched on all the time.

The internet and in particular YouTube are full of ideas on how we can all live simply and reduce our carbon footprint. Nearly all foodstuffs we discard can be recycled. For example, coffee grind is excellent for the garden, eggshells can be crushed and dug into soil to provide protein. Orange Peel can be soaked in vinegar and water to make your own detergent, the list is endless.

Take time to discover your way of helping the environment and in doing so, follow your instincts rather than the crowd.

Think about how happy you are with your impact on the environment. Is there anything further you can do to lessen your impact? If you need ideas, then try searching YouTube for "how can I reduce my carbon footprint". From the videos you watch, take just one idea and implement it straight away. Record your thoughts in the space below.

Home

"Home sweet home. This is the place to find happiness. If one doesn't find it here one doesn't find it anywhere"

M. K. Soni

Perhaps the most important personal space of all is our home, it is a place we can feel safe, shut out the world and relax. It is the space in which we can do whatever we want. Our homes should be a reflection of ourselves, our personalities, our interests and our hobbies. It should be the one place that truly reflects who we are.

When it comes to what's right and wrong, interior design-wise, the simple truth is, there is no right or wrong, it's what works for you and makes you feel happy.

There are two current popular strategies for interior design, both at opposite extremes, Minimalism and Maximalism.

Minimalists advocate the less is more principle and Maximalists the more is better. Somewhere in the middle is possibly easier to live with. Too much stuff and you can't see the wood for the trees and too little reveals nothing about who you are.

Minimalism, in my opinion, is a great lifestyle choice when you are young and moving from place to place. It gives you the freedom to move easily and frees up money which can be spent doing things or saving for future events. Integral to Minimalism is the purchase of items which are the best you can afford; in this way, it lasts longer without the need for replacement. It's also more likely you will remain happier and enjoy using the item for longer.

As we get older, we accumulate things, some of these things will remind us of an experience or have sentimental value, these things have a place in our lives. Other things serve no function and have no real place in our lives, these are things that should be moved on as they are a burden.

Editing your space should be a continuous exercise. As we pass through life, our tastes change, our income changes and technology changes. We are constantly evolving and with this, our personal spaces and homes evolve.

SHELVE Tip

Start thinking now about a style you like. Is there a particular era that appeals, have you seen a film or TV programme with an interior you have fallen in love with? Don't be afraid to dream, think out of the box. It's your unique style that no one else has, and you only have to please yourself. Record your initial thoughts in the space below and following blank page.

Finding your own unique style

Style is something each of us already has, all we need to do is find it."

Diane von Furstenberg

The clothes you wear say something about who you are, Society dictates that in certain situations we must dress according to the protocol afforded to the occasion. However, unlike clothes, your home is there to solely please you, not the world.

You don't attend an interview for a job by inviting the interviewer to your house for a home tour. So, you have complete freedom to create the home you like not the home that will impress others.

The easiest style is to follow the crowd. It's an easy style requiring very little imagination. This style is very safe as it's not particularly difficult to get wrong, it's easy to keep clean and tidy and serves a function. It's also an easy style to use if you are looking to sell your house as it creates a great first impression and rooms look bigger. So, there is nothing wrong with this style, it's just that it doesn't say anything about you.

There are many places to discover your style, a good place to start is examining Films and TV programmes, Instagram or Pinterest and making a note of what appeals.

Look at the home you live in, will it adapt to your style, what changes will you need to make?

The chances are you are already halfway to the style you want, you will most likely have collected pieces of furniture and decorated in a way that appeals to you.

Once you have decided on a style, start looking at how you can build that style up and what you need. Interior Designers use mood boards and perhaps this is something you could mock-up.

Remember you can achieve a similar look to your favourite TV, or film set by shopping smartly and buying second hand, it is not only cheaper but ethically sound.

Old furniture can be painted or repurposed creating something unique. There is something special about giving a new lease of life and home to an unloved object.
Quite often old furniture is better quality than new and will last you a lifetime if looked after. Items reach a point where they become timeless and never go out of fashion.

I have taken an old non-working valve radio, refurbished the wood and installed a modern Internet Radio into it, using the original speaker. The result was a thoroughly unique radio with fantastic sound quality. It sounds particularly good playing the British 1940s radio station. With a bit of imagination and time, you can create anything you want.

Vintys or people who live in the past will seek out pieces that suit the period they would love to live in. Some people have turned their whole homes back into time capsules of the 30s, '40s, '50s and '60s, having got that far they then find the desire to dress in the same way and drive cars from their favourite era. Some even go further, banishing modern technology from their homes or disguising it.

There is a comfort we seek in recreating the past, but it is the individual who must experiment and decide which style suits them best. Taking the radio as an example it can fit in perfectly to a 1940 or 1950s themed home and yet become a centre-piece to a modern contemporary home. It has its own elegance, a talking piece and a connection with the past.

A fundamental element of Simple Living is Quality over Quantity. This can certainly be true when buying second hand. For example, second-hand hifi is a fraction of the cost of brand new and can be much better quality. A quality receiver and speakers from the 1970s will sound better, for the same price, as its modern-day equivalent. Of course, you won't get the same features and you may have to have it repaired more often unless it's been restored, but you will enjoy your music more and have a fuller, richer sound.

When embarking on a radical change of style, find the style you like and don't be afraid to change it as you develop more, or your tastes change. Don't be tempted to just go out and buy everything of a particular style, choose carefully and choose quality.

SHELVE Tip

Start thinking now about where you are going to start with your new style, pick a room and think how you want to decorate and furnish it. Make a note in your journal of how the room will have to change to accommodate your new style, what will you need to get rid of? Can you easily make the change, or will it need more planning? Use the space below to record your thoughts.

Is there a **SHELVE Style?**

Strictly speaking, there is no such thing as a definitive SHELVE style, in the same way, there are obvious Simple Living styles such as minimalism. If there is a SHELVE style, then it would be a fusion of three different styles. The Author's favourites are Mid Century Danish Modern, Louis XV French and English Country House. I think the mix of three styles is enough to allow pieces to shine against others, without the ensemble becoming too confused. As SHELVE incorporates Hygge and Lagom the design scheme would include plenty of texture, wraps, throws, and cushions. There would be not too much of any one thing and not too little – in fact, the balance in all objects would be just about right. SHELVE Style is how you choose to combine the six lifestyle choices into a formula that works for you.

Putting Colour into your life

"Colour is a power which directly influences the soul"

Wassily Kandinsky

The problem with an approach of painting walls neutral doesn't express any individuality or personality. Don't be afraid to experiment with colour, it can add warmth and vitality to any interior.

Feature walls are a great place to start, these can be bold strong colours but if you are frightened of messing up then it is better to get some sample pots of paint and go for the lightest shade of a colour you like.

Paint tends to dry darker than the samples indicate. A lighter shade of a colour will take easier to white walls and provide a good base to repaint in a darker shade later on. If you are decorating several rooms then shades from the same pallet work well. For example, chalky pale paints in different colours complement each other but bold greens, browns, blues and reds will overwhelm.

There are common rules such as light blues can look cold, too much red will have you seeing red and green is good for studying.

A common mistake people make is to use the wrong type of paint. Walls are better with a matt finish as it dries making the wall look flat, vinyl paint will show up any flaws in plasterwork. Satin on doors and woodwork is easy to clean and doesn't show up flaws quite as much as traditional gloss paint.

Don't overlook wallpaper, it can be hung easily and creates an atmosphere.

As with everything else, the better-quality paint, wallpaper, and tools you use to decorate, the better the finish and the happier you will be with the result. Something which has been said many times is that preparation is key, so don't skimp on this part. There are hundreds of YouTube videos available to get you started if you are unsure.

An important element of Hygge is the use of Fabrics, they are key to softening a look, adding colour and creating atmosphere. They have the advantage that they can be changed easily, and you can mix and match as much as you like. A rug will instantly soften a wooden floor, cushions are easy to move around, and they can be moved easily from room to room. Throws cover up old furniture and create a bohemian look. Different textures create interest and something nice to touch or snuggle up into.

Bed linen need not be white, you can experiment with coloured or even patterned linings and coverings to suit the room.

Towels for the bathroom don't have to be white, you can mix and match and have them inject colour into the blandest of bathrooms.

Again, there is no right or wrong, buy or make what you like and enjoy the feeling of warmth and homeliness.

Art is a great way of creating impact and adding personality to a room. Hanging a French poster in a hallway instantly creates the hint of a French connection.

If you want to explore your inner creativity and cannot find paintings suitable then why not paint your own? Canvases are relatively cheap, decide on the colours you want and then what it is you are going to paint. Sketch the outline in pencil so you can easily correct any mistakes and then add the colour.
If you are more adventurous and have access to a projector, you can project an original onto your canvas and then outline in pencil before painting. This is particularly good if you want to create your own Andy Warhol type painting or recreate an old master. This technique allows you to create quite large wall art which will have a large impact on any room.

One of the nicest restaurants I've eaten in used totally mismatched china and this got me thinking that not all china needs to be white. Yes, having all your plates, mugs, cups, and saucers white makes it easy to replace pieces that break, but it is expensive and a bit bland. I started buying plates, mugs and cups from thrift stores, antique shops, and car boot sales for their design, colour and personal appeal. Now I have a very interesting eclectic collection that is unique to me.

Another example of Hygge coming into play with your home is the Danes' love of fireplaces, lighting, and candles. All designed to warm up and soften the long dark winters.

SHELVE Tip

Start thinking about colours. Are you reading this book in Winter and you need nice warm earthy colours or are you reading this in the Summer, and you want cool colours to maximise the sunlight? Cushions and throws are an easy way to experiment with colour. If you are feeling brave maybe try some paint tester pots to change the colour of rooms? Think about colours you like and which make you happy and use the space below to record your thoughts.

Hobbies

"To be really happy and safe, one ought to have at least two or three hobbies and they must all be real."

Winston Churchill

All of us need an escape from modern-day living. Life can be fast and frantic. Having a hobby is the perfect antidote and way to relax. Your hobbies can keep you on a constant learning path or they can entertain and challenge you. Almost anything can become a hobby. So long as you enjoy your hobby then it's up to you. The great thing is you can experiment with hobbies. Unlike careers and jobs, it doesn't matter too much if you make a mistake and get it wrong.

My Father taught me the importance of hobbies, he has always been a Radio Amateur and his hobby has constantly evolved as technology has changed. At 80 something he is as sharp today as he was 40 years ago, embraces technology and is never afraid to try something new. He still has a friend from his childhood who is also a "Radio Ham" and they speak every week, exchanging views, news and technology trends.

Being in the Air Force he wasn't always able to have his radio equipment set up every time we moved, so instead, he found new hobbies. Car Mechanics, building a colour TV set, HiFi, Music, Learning the Piano, Photography, Playing Rugby, Growing Vegetables even a nod to cookery at one point, although it was only a coffee cake. The point is he was never afraid to give something a go and the lessons learnt carried forward into other areas of his life and have kept his mind sharp, allowing him to enjoy and look forward to every day.

There are so many hobbies out there and some hobbies can turn into a career. Interior Design is a good example, this can lead from designing your own room to friends' rooms, word spreads and soon you have clients.

Hobbies can save you money, for example, servicing your car can not only be enjoyable but save you hundreds of pounds in garage bills.

You may find the SHELVE Facilitators offer you plenty of scope for hobbies, here is just one example from each:

Vintage Living	>	Restoring Furniture
Slow Living	>	Cooking
Simple Living	>	Growing Vegetables
Hygge	>	Dinner Parties and Entertaining
Lagom	>	Coffee and Baking Pastries
Improv	>	Amateur Dramatics

Each of the hobbies above can bring you into contact with other like-minded people who can encourage you on your journey. Most of the hobbies are of course interchangeable between the different facilitator areas and there are many, many, more for you to discover.

The main message of this section is to not be afraid to try something new, you have nothing to lose and everything to gain.

Think of a hobby you have always wanted to try and find out how you can start it. Make a point of proactively starting a new hobby. It can be anything which takes your fancy and needn't cost anything. Photographing landscapes, as an example, costs nothing and if you have a smartphone, you can use your phone as a camera. Whatever you choose, start working on it now as only you can start your hobbies and you will be the first to benefit. Use the space below to record your thoughts.

Your SHELVE Life Wheel

Now you have read this part of the book, armed with the information you have, you may want to complete your Life Choices SHELVE Wheel.

To complete your, SHELVE Life Wheel, draw a circle, and divide it into the six areas of SHELVE Life. For each category rate a mark out of ten and then place a dot in the middle of the category according to how you have rated your satisfaction with the item. So, a 10 would be the edge of the circle a five in the middle and so on. When you have ranked each item join the dots together to see how round your wheel is. The parts that are not round are the parts you need to work on.

In the example on the next page, I have rated my health as 9/10, economics 7/10. Social 6/20, environment 8/10, Home 3/10 and hobbies 9/10.

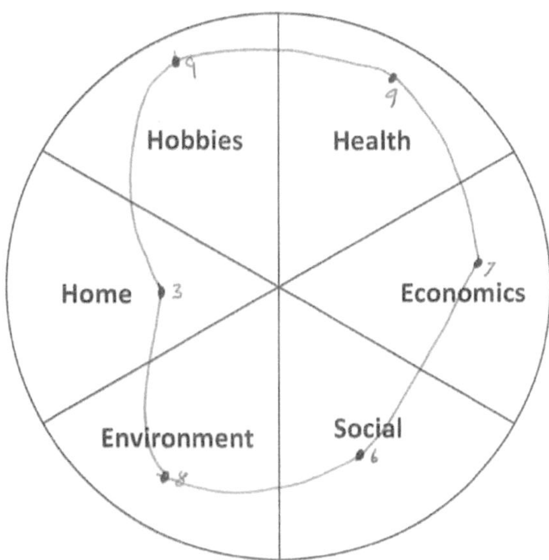

Clearly, I would be in trouble if this wheel was on the front of my bicycle. The whole machine would lean forward, and I would be hitting a flat spot whenever I hit the "home" part of the wheel.

What the wheel is telling me is that whilst my health and hobbies are great, I need to do some work firstly on my home, then my social network, then my economic situation and finally how I feel about my contribution to the environment. Ideally, I would need to get these to a 10 and then further improve my Health and Hobbies. Sometimes improving areas that are down can improve other areas through knock-on effects and as a result, you become happier and your wellbeing increases.

Keep your SHELVE Life Wheel until Part 4 when you will use it to work out your project plan.

Part 3

Facilitators

Within SHELVE there are six Facilitators, these in the main act as Tools, they can be seen as drivers, and we can take from them as much or as little as we want. They are constants and their full bandwidth is always available. So, the Facilitator circle is round.
In the analogy of the bicycle, this would be the back wheel and will go round perfectly. It is the front wheel, the life wheel, which may not be round and this is causing us a bumpy ride in life.

The Facilitator Wheel looks like this

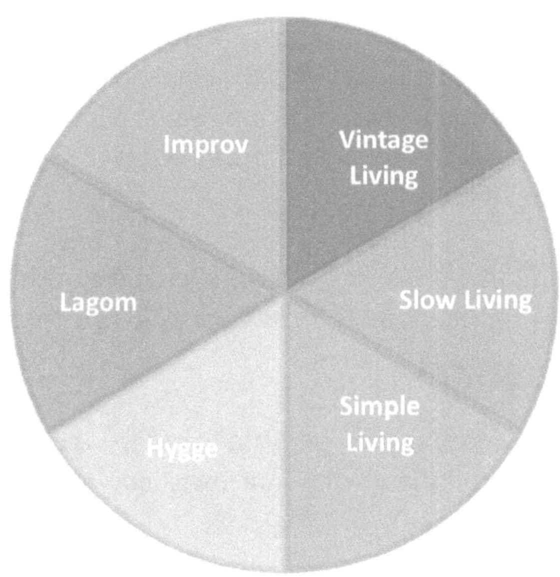

Let's look at each element in the next few pages

Vintage Living

"One should never be the oldest thing in one's house"

Patsy Stone (Absolutely Fabulous!)

Vintage Living can loosely be described as "living in the past". However, it's not quite that simple.

Vintage Living incorporates some of the best things from the past into our modern lives. Some people will find this could be as simple as cooking meals from scratch just
as their grandparents did. For others, it could be a desire to turn their home into a living, breathing replica of a past era they want to live in. They may go further and dress according to the era, some even using transport in sympathy with their vintage dream. Some Vintys choose to socialise with each other and attend mass vintage events – Goodwood Revival being a prime example.

Because in some ways living in the past was simpler and slower there are many similarities with Slow and Simple Living, it's just that the physical identification is more prominent.

Vintage Living is hugely appealing if you want to escape the modern world when you are at home and create your own individual living space, even if it is in another era.

I think the modern world has become too pressurised, chaotic, and confusing that many people (myself included) look to the past for ways to help us live today.

An interesting way in which Vintage Living can help with slowing down and living simpler is in the use of technology. Later in this book, we cover the use of Smart Phones, however simple vintage mobile phones can provide the answer to the problems some people have with smartphones. The same can be said of listening to music on Vinyl or CDs as opposed to streaming.

Interestingly Vintage Living can help make you more environmentally aware. Furniture does not have to be new, recycling together with a "make do and mend" attitude, helps reduce our carbon footprints.

When looking at a Vintage Style, don't be afraid to mix different eras, it's what appeals to you. Remember a few Antiques in a contemporary setting can look stunning and allows them to become a centrepiece.

Vintage Living can influence how you spend your money. In the past, people were more frugal in their spending habits and thought long and hard before making major purchases. Credit Cards were not even around, and a loan was something you were interviewed for.

You may want to do some more research into Vintage Living on the internet. Find out if there are elements that appeal to you and how you could incorporate them into your lifestyle. It needn't necessarily mean dressing in a vintage style, it could be adopting a more frugal food shop to help with other areas of your life. Record your thoughts on how Vintage Living could help you in the space below.

Slow Living

"Slow living isn't about determining how little we can live with – it's about working out what we simply can't live without."

Nathan Williams, The Kinfolk Home

Slow Living is the movement advocating slowing down aspects of your life to fully appreciate what's going on around you. By slowing down life you can start to live in the moment and by living in the moment you start to enjoy whatever it is you are doing, who you are with, where you are and what's around you. It is about slowing down to enjoy the journey of life rather than rushing to meet our destination.

The movement started with Slow Cooking where it was found that cooking a meal slowly over a few hours (for example a stew) brought out more flavour and nutrition rather than cooking it for an hour at 200 degrees.

A misconception about Slow Living is that it means doing everything slowly, this is wrong, it is simply that you do things at a pace that gives you time to appreciate and enjoy what you are doing. If you look at the work environment, so many people think by working late and appearing 100% busy the whole time, they are efficient. This is not true. From my own experience, the people who appear busy the whole time are people unable to make the best use of their time and are nowhere near as productive as other colleagues. To be successful in business you must always build in contingency, whether it's your budget or your time. If you build in time contingency to your day, you will be better placed to deal with unexpected issues without impacting the rest of your work. If you don't then you deal with unexpected issues on the fly and are unable to resolve them properly, leading to greater issues in the long run.

I worked somewhere once where they published, for all to see, the hours each person worked in a week. It was so obvious that some people couldn't possibly have worked the hours they did, they just said they did as they thought it would make them look super productive and super dedicated. To me, this was a clear sign they were unable to manage their time and realistically plan their workload with their manager. This was born out later as these people were the ones who appeared stressed and made poor business decisions. At the same organisation we had a policy of open electronic diaries, the people who in my mind were poor managers of their time, had booked back-to-back meetings this giving the impression they were super busy. Again, this is poor business practice as you are leaving yourself no time to catch up on email and action anything assigned to you.

People following a Slow Living routine, will inevitably spend a great deal of time organising themselves so they make the best possible use of their time. Slow Living means being able to say no to things you don't want to do and enjoy the things you do want to do. Slow living means building in contingency.

Because Slow Living is about living in the moment, people who follow this lifestyle set low expectations, in this way disappointment is unlikely. Set high expectations too high and you will be disappointed if you don't meet your goals.

Slow Living people make more time for their hobbies and quite often these hobbies relate to the Environment and being close to nature. There is nothing better than planting your own vegetables, waiting for them to grow, harvesting them, and then cooking a meal. Another connection to the environment is in mindful consumption, that is consuming less, not buying things for the sake of acquisition and thereby spending money unnecessarily. This means purchase decisions are often based on the need for the item and buying the best quality within the budget so the item lasts longer and is nicer to use.

Identify one area of your life you would like more time to enjoy and slow down. Next, identify an area of your life you would happily do faster giving you more time to enjoy the area you enjoy. Be creative in your thinking, maybe you like cooking but hate hoovering – can someone else do the hoovering and reward them with a nice meal or loaf of bread? Can you get one of those robot machines to do it for you? Can you make less mess so you don't need to hoover as often? It doesn't matter how outlandish your ideas appear as being creative and thinking outside the box will often yield the best ideas. Use the space below to record your thoughts.

Simple Living

"Simplicity is the ultimate sophistication"

Leonardo Da Vinci

Simple Living focuses on ways of making life simpler, so this could be by reducing the number of possessions you have, reducing debt, living sustainably, reducing the amount of contact you have with people you don't like or reducing your journey time to work to make life simpler.

Simple Living naturally aligns itself to minimalism, but it doesn't have to. For example, Simple Living in my opinion can also be aligned closely with Vintage Living which does not advocate living a minimalist life. Take for example someone wishing to live a 1940s life, possessions and home will be simple but hardly minimal, however, food and health will focus around living simply and frugally.

An overwhelmingly large part of Simple Living is Decluttering. Decluttering can also serve to clear the decks for Slow and Vintage Living and so it's why this is now covered at length here.

Decluttering

"The first step in crafting the life you want is to get rid of everything you don't"

Joshua Becker

Our lives are full of three types of stuff. Physical, Non-Physical, and Emotional. Physical stuff is the things we can see, books, furniture, magazines, clothes etc. Non-physical and emotional stuff is the things we cannot see and incorporate emotional baggage - e-mail, forums, social media, debt, relationships etc.

Decluttering all areas of our lives is important not only to our mental health, but our finances, homes, and our general wellbeing.

Swedish Death Cleaning

Swedish Death Cleaning (SDC) or, Döstädning in Swedish shouldn't be thought of as morbid! it was in fact an established practice carried out in Sweden when you felt the time in life had come for you to sort out your affairs before you passed on into the next life. The practice meant that you took responsibility for making sure your affairs were in order and you didn't leave a burden for other people to sort out. Typically, one would call on friends and family to come round and take possessions they no longer needed.

This traditional practice has been updated by Margaretta Magnusson and is detailed in her book "The Gentle Art of Swedish Death Cleaning".

The difference between the traditional practice and the modern practice is that SDC is carried out when you are much younger and thus becomes a part of everyday life rather than leaving it until you are much older.

In the book Magnusson details seven important steps these are:

1.   Let your family and friends know what you are upto
2.   Start with less personal items
3.   Gift possessions away gradually
4.   Keep mementos for yourself
5.   Donate and sell the rest
6.   Make a list of important documents and passwords
7.   Declutter regularly

Key takeaways I found useful from SDC are:

- It can be useful in decluttering to give things away to friends and family that you no longer need but which you know they would find useful
- It is good practice to make sure you have documented your digital life and have this in order
- The "red dot" system. When deciding what to declutter, place a small red dot sticker on items you do not want to keep and a green one on those you do
- SDC provides a good excuse to clear out any items you may not want others to find
- Decluttering regularly is key to maintaining a clutter-free life

I highly recommend reading this book but would caveat against getting carried away and getting rid of things you may regret later in life.

Start thinking about areas of your life that are cluttered and write them in the space below. The following pages will arm you with helpful advice on how to declutter.

Physical Stuff

Physical stuff is as hard to declutter as non-physical or emotional stuff. The lines blur, when we find we keep things out of sentimentality or because it reminds us of something, someone or a moment in our lives.

If an item serves a function, you find it beautiful or you have a particular association with it, you should keep it.

We don't need to live in sterile homes with no hint of our personalities, but, by the same token, it's not particularly nice or easy to live in a home that looks like a secondhand junk shop. Too much stuff and it is difficult to appreciate the beauty within each item. It's also next to impossible to look after objects, keep them clean and in a good state of repair.

There are extremes of decluttering leaving you with barely anything other than essentials, or there is the approach of a well thought out, planned physical detox for your home.

I'll tackle each room of a house detox in turn.

Bedroom

A comfortable bedroom free of distractions makes an excellent starting point in helping you get a good night's sleep. Wardrobes full of clothes, shoes, accessories and bursting at the seams do not make for a peaceful sanctuary in which to escape the world

So, a good place to start is with your wardrobe. Go through and look at what clothes you need, and which clothes are just taking up space in case they are needed, and we get a really hot or cold spell. Are those mountain boots sat in the corner waiting for thick snow necessary? Or are you more likely to stay in by the fire and shop on the internet than risk breaking your neck in the snow?

Those old clothes which have lost their shape and make you feel scruffy, is now the time for them to go?

Clothes that no longer fit but are kept in case you lose weight you may want to get rid of as it would be nicer to treat yourself to something newer and smarter when the weight is gone. Unless of course, you have a wardrobe full of classic or vintage designer clothes, in which case you may want to keep your favourites and sell the rest.

If you really cannot bear to get rid of old clothes, then try putting them away for six months and see if you miss them.

Something you may want to consider is to match clothes to outfits. Each piece of clothing should go with three outfits. So, a pair of jeans, trousers, or skirt, for example, can be worn with a T-Shirt, and Trainers for a casual look, add a jacket for a slightly more formal look or a shirt, jacket, and smart shoes for a formal look. Once you start looking at pairing clothes with outfits and have three or four looks in mind, it is easy to then start Paring down your wardrobe leaving you free to concentrate on replacing items you don't like with longer-lasting quality items.

If you need a lot of clothes, say for work, sports, and other activities now is a good time to get organised and divide them by function. All your work clothes could be in one space and leisure clothes in another area. In this way, the lines do not blur, and you can find clothes easily and recognise what's worn out and needs to be replaced.

Organising your wardrobe properly means everything should have a space of its own and be easy to get to.

Once you have gone through your clothes you may find you have enough space to store other items you don't use very often such as holiday or leisure stuff. Or you might find you do not need as much storage allowing you to create more space in which to relax.

Whilst in the bedroom look at how much bedding you have in stock, if there is too much perhaps some of it can be given away or cut up and used as dusters?

Having organised clothes and laundry, clear out any clutter and consider what it is you need in a bedroom to get to sleep.

Do you need to have your phone on charge next to your bed? Probably not, if your excuse is you use it as an alarm clock then consider buying an alarm clock. Do you need to stay up late watching TV, no, maybe that could be moved out too?

If space is tight and you have a workspace or desk in your bedroom which cannot be moved or is there because the room is a quiet place in which to work, then look at creative solutions to disguise it.
Having cleared wardrobe space, perhaps your home office could be installed in a wardrobe so you can't see it when you are going to sleep, or can you make a screen to go round it when not in use?
If you are lucky enough to have a fireplace in your bedroom you could always have one side as a wardrobe and the other as a workspace with curtains unifying the space but hiding clothes and work equipment.

Sitting Room

The sitting room is the room in the house we invite most people into. It should reflect who we are but at the same time be clean and tidy, but not so overwhelming sterile that it is uncomfortable to spend any length of time in.

If you have bookcases with loads of books, records and CDs then go through and remove those you no longer read or listen to and are never likely to want to use again. I have a lot of books and records, but they are all ones I want to keep. When I was decluttering, I gave books and records I didn't need any more to a Thrift Store. Getting rid of the excess has made it easier for me to find the books and records I want when I need them.

Apply the same technique of reviewing what you have to ornaments, pictures, photographs, electronic devices, lamps etc. Gather everything together and box it all up. Maybe leave it in your newly found wardrobe space for three months and see if you miss it? If not then it's time to go, if you do miss it, then put it back.

Look at the furniture you have, do you have too much? If you have too much, then think about paring it down to your favourite pieces. If you don't like a piece, then start looking for pieces that suit your style and use what you have until you can get what you really want.

You could write down your plans and use them as a goal so you are committed to the change. It is pointless living long term with things you don't need or like. It is much better to get something you want and give away something you don't want than it is to hang onto it because it either cost too much or is too much trouble to get rid of.

No one else can change your furniture for you, this is something only you can do, but it is your opportunity to create the look you want.

These days TV sets are massive, and furniture tends to be arranged around the TV, consider instead disguising your TV by hanging it on the wall with artwork around it, or, installing it in a cabinet so it is out of sight when not in use. An alternative to a TV is a projector which can be mounted on the ceiling and projected onto a pull-down blind or projector screen. The advantage of a projector is that it is much more discreet and provides movie theatre-like viewing. With a TV out of the way, you have room to arrange your room for event viewing or entertaining guests comfortably.

In small spaces, multifunctional furniture is invaluable, sofas that can become beds, coffee tables that turn into dining tables and chairs that can be deflated or folded away, the list is endless and it's time to get creative when thinking about how you use your room and how you will furnish it.

One exercise I've heard of is to pack up absolutely everything and then live with nothing for a while, after a few weeks start moving back the things you really need. This is great if you have loads of space and don't mind packing and unpacking, but for most of us, we don't have the space and would rather be doing other things.

Kitchen

Decluttering a kitchen might seem like an easy task - just clear the worktops and remove anything that looks like it has nothing to do with cooking. The reality is there are far more factors to be considered and it is not a one size fits all.

Some people love cooking and want a cook's kitchen with pots and pans hanging down and oils and spices out on display. These kitchens are used all the time and are a fun place to be. Other people have no interest in cooking and use their kitchen counters to serve up drinks and canapés, a large fridge is essential to store party supplies. These kitchens to their owners and guests are just as much fun as they fulfil a function and are nice places to spend time in.

Other factors coming into consideration are the size of your kitchen, how much cupboard space you have, what type of cooking you do and what type of style you like - do you want to be minimalist, maximalist, or somewhere in the middle.

Somewhere in the middle and making the best of what's there is most likely to be the most common approach and the reason why minimalist or maximalist won't work in a normal kitchen.

One of the reasons why it is difficult to restyle a kitchen to a minimalist style is that if you remove everything and have completely clear surfaces you highlight everything wrong with the kitchen, the hob which has marks, the worktop with stains, the worn cooker hood, the tiles that are out of date and need to be replaced.

The sleek "high end" minimalist look works best where the kitchen has been designed to look minimalist from the very outset or is brand new, both these options usually cost vast sums of money.

You can however achieve a minimalist kitchen by replacing cupboards with shelves and paring down the amount of crockery and ingredients you have on the shelves. Walls could be painted white, and a wooden worktop would add warmth.

Taking the maximalist approach to kitchens works in a country cottage setting but not in a loft apartment or three-bed suburban semi. The same is true of themed kitchens. I would love a French kitchen, but I don't live in France and so it will always be a kitchen in a normal house trying to be French. Whereas my approach has been to hint at a French-style rather than go overboard with hanging garlic, strategically placed olive oil, French bread and wicker baskets.

My approach to decluttering a kitchen is to empty it, give everything a deep thorough clean, mentally organise and plan how you will use the kitchen, then move back in.

Ideally, you will have somewhere to store all the stuff you take out of the kitchen, for example, put things into baskets and in another room out of the way during the process.

Starting with foodstuffs, go through absolutely everything, tinned food, the fridge, frozen food, spices etc. Throw away everything out of date. Now refine the process and go through everything again but looking at the foodstuffs you will use and that you enjoy. If you are starting on a diet this is a great time to clear out all "bad" foods.

Any unwanted in date food can be donated to a Food Bank rather than thrown away. In this way, you are helping someone else out.

Ok, so now it is time to look at Cooking Appliances, which ones simply take up cupboard or counter space and are never used. They are the first to go in the thrift box. Do the same with pots, pans, bowls, cutlery.

Many of us are seduced into buying stuff we don't need or use, it ends up cluttering our spaces and serves no function. Worst you could buy something expensive like a food processor and never use it. Bear in mind the type of kitchen you want, if you have a grill and make very little toast, do you need a toaster? Do you want a stovetop kettle or an electric kettle? Do you need three different types of coffee machines? Do you really need a panini maker or can it double as a grill?

Expensive mistakes can be sold on the secondhand market or given to friends and relatives - the important thing is to recognise it was a mistake and move on. You won't cleanse your mind and move on if it is still in the cupboard reminding you that you once wasted money on it.

At one time I had a multitude of cooking pans and ovenware. The problem was I thought I needed so many different types to be able to cook properly. Invariably having too many meant I kept old and dirty ovenware past its sell-by date. I also ended up with way too many cast iron pots. One large pan is usually enough for cooking meats, making chilli con carne, spaghetti, or stews. Cheap oven trays rarely last and you can end up buying more than you need as they wear quickly. Go through and work out what you need, discard those that are worn or are not used, and you should be left with good quality items which will get used frequently. As they fail replace with better quality.

Now is the time to get rid of any chipped or broken tableware. If you want to achieve a more minimalist kitchen then consider how many plates, mugs, bowls and saucers you need. This is going to vary, if you have a big family then you need more. If you have a dishwasher then you need quite a lot anyway, but if you live in a small flat on your own and have friends around every other week then you need much less. Six of everything would work in that setting. A four-person household could survive on six of everything as a minimum but with guests and a dishwasher twelve would be more practical.

Again, it is better to have china you love and will enjoy using rather than have stuff filling a cupboard.

There used to be a time when people had very large collections of glasses, they would have glasses for wine, champagne, brandy, shorts, whisky, gin and tonic etc. etc. Over time fashion has changed and with it the glasses. Champagne glasses somehow narrowed and turned into flutes, wine glasses grew at the same rate as cars, becoming taller and fatter.

If you have lots of space and enjoy entertaining then having lots of glasses can be useful, if not then look at what you need. If you have a small space, then a minimum would be a few tall glasses and some tumblers which can be used for alcoholic and non-alcoholic drinks. If you are trying to cut back on alcohol, then get rid of these types of glasses as they only serve as a prompt or trigger to drink alcohol. If you think you may need them in the future box them up and store them.

By now you will have noticed that in simplifying life we start to look more objectively at how objects are used and, multifunctional objects of good quality are favoured over single-use poor quality items.

Before moving back into your kitchen, take some time to give it a proper deep clean.

Once your kitchen is clean think about how you are going to use it. Which items do you use daily, and which do you use maybe once a week or once in a blue moon? Think about how your kitchen operates. Here are some tips for making your kitchen work for you:

Worktops should accommodate frequently used electrical items. This saves them from being taken in and out of cupboards and frequent plugging and unplugging. All of which increases the risk of damaging them.

If you are short of cupboard space, oils and spices can be stored on trays or in baskets on the worktop. This helps create the look of a cook's kitchen.

Try and group items near the activity they perform. I bake my own bread, so it is good having the food mixer and bread-making equipment all in one place, besides which the food mixer is heavy, and I tend not to use it if it is stored in a cupboard.

Consider having your kettle on a surface near the sink with mugs and tea coffee etc. in a cupboard above it.

Store dishes and plates near your dishwasher or sink. It makes putting them away much quicker and easier.

If you want to create the look of a minimalist but stylish kitchen then consider decanting things like rice, pasta and cereals into jars and create your own labels.

Decanting means you can save money buying refill portions of the contents rather than the prepackaged variety. Visually decanting into personalised containers is more appealing and makes it easy to find items.

Make your kitchen work for you and it will become a pleasure to prepare delicious healthy meals in.

Bathroom

Bathrooms serve two main purposes; they are the places we prepare ourselves in for the day ahead and the place we relax in at the end of the day with a shower or bath.

They should always be clean and places you want to spend time in rather than visit in a hurry to get yourself clean.

The same principles used in the kitchen apply to the bathroom, firstly clear everything out and then give the room a deep clean.

Before moving things back in consider what it is you want in there. Bathroom scales, laundry baskets and towels are obvious candidates for scrutiny. Do they work well, do you like them or are they worn out and time you replaced them?

Of course, you may have to make compromises in that these can be expensive items, but worn-out hard towels would be first on my priority. White towels create a boutique hotel look but coloured towels inject life and vibrancy, particularly if your bathroom is white or grey. Pick a colour you like and which will make you feel good.

Now your bathroom cabinet is empty think carefully before placing everything back in,
go through and dispose of empty items and think about what you want to keep in there.
The aim is to organise the cabinet so things are easy to get to and not overly cluttered. It's common sense but grouping items together by function makes it easier to find them.

Consider the use of multifunctional items. The use of a good Rose-hip and Avocado oil moisturiser can replace day, night, hand and hair creams. Used in very small quantities it lasts forever, takes up little space and saves you money in the long run. Or you could always create your own using natural ingredients.

To keep sinks and showers clean, consider buying soap dispensers as these pump out only the amount you need and don't leave messy residue on surfaces. An added benefit is you can replenish them with refill packets rather than prepackaged plastic. Visually these types of dispensers are more appealing since they are not adorned with the mass marketing. You may want to mix different hand washes to create your own unique scent.

Just as the Bedroom is a sanctuary your Bathroom should be the place you prepare for the day ahead and your wind down, prepare for bed, place in the evening. The use of texture, colour, lighting and scent with candles, together with a choice of accessories allows you to make your bathroom unique to you.

Garages, Sheds and Attics

If you are lucky enough to own a garage then the chances are you don't keep your car in it, instead, it has become a dumping ground for everything which doesn't have a home. Garages if used as dumping grounds can quickly become wasted spaces. The same is true of sheds and attics.

Cars seem to have grown over the past few years to the extent that garages are usually too small for them. If your car does fit into your garage, then there are huge advantages to keeping it there. Your car is protected from the elements and vandals, so it is likely to last longer. Neighbours and thieves are unlikely to know if you are in or out. Finally, there is a greater chance of you cycling or walking to the shops if your car is not directly outside your house.

To clear your shed, garage or attic, use the same process as the Kitchen, move everything out and go through what you need. Organise tools and garden equipment and get rid of anything out of date or no longer used.

If you do start with decluttering your garage, shed or attic first, you will have somewhere to store items you are not sure of disposing of whilst decluttering the rest of your house.

Summary

Nearly everything you don't want, someone else will. Thrift stores are crying out for good quality clothing and there are plenty of recycling bins around that will see the clothes go to someone in need. If you have expensive clothes, you no longer need, try selling them through one of the online selling platforms and raise some cash.

The trick when selling things is to not go out and immediately replace it – this just serves to clutter life up again. Better to wait until you see something you want and buy the best quality you can afford. Buying quality, not necessarily designer means it will last longer and look good for longer. It's also kinder to the environment and in the long run to your pocket.

In summary, it's ok to have things provided they serve a purpose; you like them, or they are just something you enjoy looking at and gives you pleasure. If they don't fulfil that criterion, then they serve no purpose and are better gone.

SHELVE Tip

Look back at your journal to the notes on your style and what needs to change to accommodate a new style, can any of the decluttering tips above help you in forming a plan later?

Use the space below to record your thoughts.

Non-Physical Stuff

Surprisingly we all have a lot of non-physical clutter in our lives. Non-physical clutter we can't pick up with our hands or see as a physical entity.

Some examples of Non-Physical stuff are:

* The News
* Relationships
* Digital Media – Photographs, E-Mail, Electronic Documents etc. etc.
* Social Media, Facebook, Twitter, Instagram
* Television and Radio Programmes
* Apps on Phones and Tablets
* Software Programs
* Appointments
* Arguments
* Toxic Relationships
* Threat of world disasters

As there is a great deal of fusion between the different SHELVE areas, you will notice we have already covered News, Toxic Relationships and Emotional clutter within other topics in this book. This section, therefore, deals with Digital Media

Just as in other areas of life your digital footprint can become cluttered and disorganised making it difficult to find information, photographs, e-books, contacts, documents, spreadsheets etc.

Smartphones

"We get one of these little pings on our smartphones, and we get a little hit of dopamine as well. We get excited, we feel anticipation. As we feel this, we want it more and more. So, we spend more and more time looking at our phones"

Kim Stoltz

I found the best place to start decluttering nonphysical entities is with the thing we use most often, our smartphones.

Smartphones are amazing pieces of technology and can simplify life, for example, one smartphone can replace a wallet, camera, sat-nav, music player and calculator.

Some Simple Living or Minimalism advocates will tell you that you don't need a smartphone and can get along quite happily with a simple flip phone.

Whilst that's true and if you can that's great, smartphones offer a lot of functionality and convenience. But they can end up taking over our lives.

According to an American Study by Asurion, Americans look at their smartphones 96 times a day, that's once every ten minutes. This means every ten minutes you are distracted from what you are doing. No wonder it is difficult to concentrate and enjoy life.

I found that by viewing my phone as a tool to help me, I started to rely less and less on it being close to me twenty-four seven. I changed my relationship with my phone, it was no longer the thing that I couldn't be without, it became the thing that helped me when I needed it on my terms.

I started to declutter my phone by removing anything to do with online shopping. Any app that you remove and find you need later can always be reinstalled. By removing online shopping, I found I stopped ordering things on impulse. I had to login to my computer, search for the item and then order. The time spent doing this made me think if I needed the item or if it was just a nice thing to have.

Next to go were the News Apps, they served to only add worry and stress to my daily life. I only use social media on my computer, so this wasn't a problem. I removed E-Mail as I can check it on my computer when I have the time to read and reply properly.

By the time I had finished, I was left with Maps which I find invaluable for getting to places. My Music, Is an App to control my HiFi, Internet Banking and the usual stuff like Texting, Contacts, Diary, Notes, Browser and Photographs.

By removing the non-essential apps distracting you, you can concentrate on taking a photograph or listening to some music. You are not distracted by social media, email or having to check the news. What is the point of sitting on a beautiful beach listening to your favourite music and then getting wound up by a work email or a piece of bad news – there's nothing you can do about it so why have it ruin those special moments you have to yourself?

My phone now sits in a cradle in the hall and is ready to use if I go out. The battery lasts longer, and I don't feel beholden to it.

Look at the apps on your phone, do you need them all? Try and keep a record of how many times a day you look at your phone. Work out what you need on your phone and what it is that is just nice to have but becomes a distraction. Try switching your phone off for a couple of hours when you have an important task to complete.
Use the space below to record any notes.

Electronic Media

"I'm not big on to-do lists. Instead, I use email and desktop calendars and my online calendar. So when I walk up to my desk, I can focus on the emails I've flagged and check the folders that are monitoring particular projects and particular blogs"

Bill Gates

Most of us are reliant on computers in our daily lives, sometimes be it for work, personal use or any voluntary work we are involved in.

Unlike Physical De-cluttering, Electronic decluttering does not necessarily have to mean deleting loads of files, emails and photographs. Media storage is now incredibly cheap and cloud storage solutions mean we no longer have to back up our files unless they are stored on local hard drives.

Electronic Media decluttering is focused therefore on organisation, unsubscribing and unfriending. Making it easier to find files, being a member of groups that are relevant and being friends with people you know and who you are interested in.

Electronic Documents

Perhaps the best way of thinking about how and where you store your documents is to view storage as a hierarchy. At the top level, you have where your files are stored. This could be locally on your computer's hard drive or in the cloud. Where you store your files is up to you. I store my work documents separately from my personal documents in two separate cloud locations. Within each cloud area, there is another hierarchy based on the type of files. So, work files for example have four high-level directories – Projects, Information, Documents, Archive. Within each of these, I then have further directories for each project. The Archive folder serves as a place to store everything I have finished with. By keeping the number of high-level directories low and expanding within lower levels you create a system that is easy to navigate and easy to store files in.

Take some time to think about your directory structure, can you reorganise it better now? Your directory structure may be fine as it is and you just need to have a tidy up.

Always keep an archive folder to store any files you don't use now but may need in the future. As storage is cheap you can always set yourself a 5-, 10- or 20-year rule to keep files for.

Music and Photographs

I used to regularly clear down old photographs and music from my computer, however, I now find I wish I hadn't, and I could refer back to some old photographs. As storage is so affordable, I wouldn't necessarily advocate deleting great chunks of your life in the form of digital photographs, better to archive for another day. Obvious duplicated or poor-quality photographs and music should be deleted making it easier to find good quality content.

Desktops

Having organised your directory structure now is the time to move any files from your desktop into their directories. Make a point of storing documents in their directories and not on your desktop.

Desktops should only contain shortcuts to the items you use the most often, these can be shortcuts to directories and applications. Remove any shortcuts you don't use regularly so you are left with a nice clean desktop that is easy to navigate.

Whilst looking at your desktop, don't forget to check your recycle bin is emptied regularly. All too often these can become full of old files which will slow your computer down.

Applications

Have a look through all the Applications on your computer and uninstall any you don't use; these could be games you no longer play or applications you downloaded and previously used but haven't used in a long while. This will make switching to new machines easier and potentially help speed up any software upgrades. If you are unsure on whether or not to delete an application, check first either by searching on the internet for help on deleting the app or through someone you know with IT knowledge.

Email

Legal requirements for the retention of email vary from country to country and industry to industry, you should always check with your organisation on the legal retention requirements before deleting any work emails you may require later.

One of the easiest ways to start decluttering email is to look through your emails and unsubscribe from any forums you no longer visit or require information from, then you are safe to delete these emails.

Generally, I organise my email into high-level folders, I keep emails needing to be actioned or replied to in my inbox and then move them to the relevant folder once I have responded or an issue is closed. Other people may find keeping emails organised in a folder by organisation or customer easier. A general rule though is to limit the number of emails kept in your inbox; this will make it easier to identify new urgent emails as they come in. You may decide to have a simple email folder structure of Urgent, Non-Urgent, Delegate, Not Important and Archive to deal with your mail. Find a system that works for you. Everyone has different requirements and there is not a one size fits all solution to organising email. You will however find that the mindset of Simple Living and detoxing other areas of your life will help you develop your own methods of digital organisation.

Part of a successful Digital Detox is to spend time looking at all the sites you have registered with, either on forums, social media, or shopping. You may find these are stored alongside passwords on your machine or within the history file of your machine. Go through and deregister from any sites you no longer use.

Look at your social media accounts and decide which ones you enjoy using and are of benefit to you. Go through your friends list and decide if you need to be friends with people you don't really know or if you would prefer to be friends with people you know and are genuinely interested in. Leave groups that serve no benefit. Finally, check your privacy settings to ensure they are providing you with adequate protection.

If you shop a lot on the internet, go through and check you don't have any redundant accounts containing your bank card details, limit your accounts to the ones you use regularly.

Now is a good time to look at your bookmarks and delete any unwanted ones so you are left with bookmarks for the sites you use most often.

Finally, don't forget to check your downloads folder, any downloads you no longer need, delete.

There are other measures you could take such as defragging your hard drive and clearing out old upgrade files, however, I would recommend speaking to an IT specialist first unless you feel confident carrying out the work.

SHELVE Tip

Monitor your emails daily and unsubscribe from lists you are no longer interested in. This is an easy, fast way to limit the number of spam emails you receive.

Hygge

"Be happy in the moment, that's enough. Each moment is all we need, not more"

Mother Theresa

Hygge pronounced (Hue-Guh) is the Danish way to live well. Since the Danes are amongst the happiest people on our planet and Hygge is often talked about as a contributory factor, what exactly then, is Hygge?

Hygge is not one physical state, instead, it is a way of creating an atmosphere with the use of people, objects, fabrics, music, colour etc.

The Hygge Manifesto consists of:

Atmosphere	Lighting, Candles, Fireplaces
Presence	Be in the now, eliminate distractions and concentrate on the people or task in hand
Pleasure	Comfort food, drinks, and music
Equality	Everyone in the group is equal, share and share alike in all things
Gratitude	Be grateful for having this time together
Harmony	No need for competition between true friends
Comfort	Relax, wear comfortable clothes like soft woolen jumpers and wooly socks, use throws and comfortable cushions to snuggle up into
Truce	Avoid contentious topics of conversation

Togetherness	It's about building memories and recalling old times
Shelter	You are with friends; you can feel safe

Denmark experiences dark and cold winters, something most people dread, but the Danes will light rooms with soft lamps or candles, wear comfortable warm clothes and use rugs and cushions to create a cosy atmosphere. The Danes love creating intimate warm living spaces which can be shared with their families and friends.

According to one report, Danes consume the most candles per head of population in Europe, they are also very keen on Fireplaces. Fires being very Hygge.

Hygge can also be practised on your own, there is no reason why you shouldn't for example take time out during the day to have a Hygge moment. Maybe this is sitting looking out of a window with a warm shawl around you, the fire lit and sipping a cup of tea with just silence in the background. It's your time to yourself and a time to reflect.

Don't feel you can't practice Hygge because you don't have candles or a fireplace. A low energy bulb, 2 W 2000K or thereabouts will give a warm glow. An electric fireplace will give focus to a room and provide that all-important warm glow.

As you discover more about Hygge you will see how it relates to many different aspects of life areas within the SHELVE methodology.

SHELVE Tips

Practice taking time out to have a Hygge moment all to yourself.

Create a Hygge Corner in your home, start with your favourite chair, a cushion and a warm blanket. Make this a place where you go to read with a cup of freshly brewed tea. If you want to take things a stage further, make a point of switching your phone off and have a proper digital 20-minute detox.

Start keeping a record of your Hygge moments here and record how you feel after them. Is this something you are going to maintain?

Lagom

"He who buys what he does not need, steals from himself"

Swedish Proverb

Lagom is the Swedish word meaning "not too much, and not too little" or "just the right amount". Lagom is more less the same as Sopivasti in Finnish and Passelig in Norwegian. All of these words roughly translate into Moderation, Just Right, Suitable, Appropriate or Ample.

The Lagom concept stems back to the Vikings and their gatherings around a fire in the evening. They would often drink mead from a horn, passing it from one person to the next. They all knew that if they drank too much someone else may not get a drink. This concept of not taking too much or too little is still prevalent in Swedish society whereby all citizens pay sufficient tax to ensure everyone enjoys a relatively good standard of life and there are no extremes of wealth or poverty. It is perhaps one of the many reasons why the Swedes, like the Danes, are said to be amongst the happiest people in the world.

The Swedish Lagom concept accepts there is no such thing as Perfectionism and nothing can be perfect, instead, it focuses on accepting there are imperfections in life and focus instead on the moments of joy within our lives. An extension of this is to accept the mistakes we have made in the past and focus instead on the future. Everyone has made mistakes in their past and will have made decisions they regret, but there is absolutely nothing that can be done about it, instead, it is healthier to focus on the future rather than go over the past.

"Do Fika" – Fika is the Swedish for taking a break from tasks in order to socialise. The Swedes make a point of having a ten-minute coffee break at work with their colleagues to talk and catch up. This is sometimes accompanied by a pastry such as a Cinnamon bun. In the UK, an old tradition, now reserved for formal occasions, is Afternoon Tea. I believe we should reintroduce this as a mainstream activity in the same way as the Swedish do Fika.

Lagom as a methodology encourages you to simplify elements of your life so you have not too much or too little of any one thing. In reality, this means, for example with money, it is good to have enough money to live comfortably, but too much money can present problems with looking after it and too little money creates other problems.

Lagom can be applied to nearly every aspect of our lives. Too many friends and we don't form close partnerships, too few friends and we become a closed circle which is hard to break into. Too big a house and we have high bills; too small a house and we don't have room to breathe.

An important lesson Lagom teaches us is, we cannot change the past, but we can look forward to the future, and, if we let ourselves look forward to the future then we can plan and dream, and, with that will come moments of joy we will remember forever.

Lagom encourages you to slow down, so you can start to appreciate a life based on moderation, sustainability, and awareness of others. Swedes tend to have fewer mental health problems due to stress; this is because rather than wait to become stressed the Swedes will deal with the issue straight away and take a break away from work.

Sweden has long championed the Work/Life balance the rest of Europe is just getting to grips with. If you deal with the cause of stress straight away, you will become more productive in the long run. Spending long hours at work does not guarantee productivity or efficiency, what it does guarantee is you will be worn out and stressed much quicker and less able to perform to the best of your ability.

There are many elements of Lagom incorporated within the SHELVE methodology, for example saying no, setting realistic goals and decluttering.

SHELVE Tip

If you are constantly having to work late, try leaving work early and relaxing, switch off from work, then start the next day by planning your day ahead. If you are still stressed, speak to your manager and explain how you feel.

Use the space below to record your thoughts.

Improv

"Reinvent new combinations of what you already own. Improvise. Become more creative. Not because you have to, but because you want to. Evolution is the secret for the next step."

Karl Lagerfeld

Improv or Improvisation in its strictest interpretation is a form of theatre whereby the performance is unplanned and unscripted. It gives the actors complete freedom to go with whatever they happen to think at the time and whichever random way the storyline is headed. No one knows the ending as it hasn't been scripted.

The reason why Improv is included in SHELVE as a Facilitator is because, much like improv on the stage, life is also unscripted and none of us knows the ending, but we can control our direction through our life choices and actions.

Improv within the SHELVE setting is about feeling free to take action, to look at life differently, realise our dreams and be daring. It's about doing the unexpected to live a life less ordinary.

Think about a time you did something outlandish or out of character, was it fun? how did it make you feel? Would you do it again? If not, why not? How could you change the action? Use the space below to record your thoughts.

The Inner Game

"The player of the inner game comes to value the art of relaxed concentration above all other skills; he discovers a true basis for self-confidence; and he learns that the secret to winning any game lies in not trying too hard."

W. Timothy Gallwey

W. Timothy Gallwey is best known for writing a book called "The Inner Game of Golf", in this book he discusses how the mental approach to golf is just as important as the physical approach. Gallwey's technique is to allow the golfer to concentrate solely on hitting the ball, rather than where to hit it and worry about angles etc. He found that golfers going back to basics and concentrating on hitting the ball achieved better results than those worrying about the technical aspects. This technique was then used by coaches in other sports to great success.

Time to be a child again

The secret of genius is to carry the spirit of the child into old age which means never losing your enthusiasm."

Aldous Huxley

The inner game can be likened to how we are as children. As children we are not afraid to try new things, we learn quickly and acquire new skills rapidly. This is because we are not afraid of what people will think of us, we are concerned with accomplishing the task and moving on to the next thing. We haven't yet had the life experiences of an adult and faced disappointment or humiliation.

After reading "the inner game" I decided I would apply Gallwey's technique to sailing. For years, I had problems getting in and out of Pontoons as I thought too much about what the wind and tide were doing, how quickly should I turn, how much power should I use. I found that by clearing my mind of these things, I was able to concentrate on what the boat was doing and "feel" based on how strong the wind and tide were when to turn and how much power to use. This was revolutionary to me and the more I practised the better I got. The better I got the more confidence I gained and so on.

I then tried this technique with piano playing. I found that instead of concentrating so hard on the technicalities of playing the piano, and, instead on relaxing and enjoying what I was doing, I was able to play much better and again this inspired confidence leading to better playing.

Sometimes we need to try, not try so hard, give ourselves a break and rediscover the enthusiasm we had as children for trying new things.

SHELVE Tip

Is there a task you have trouble completing because it requires a higher level of skill than you currently have? Try and relax the next time you do the task and let your mind think about completing the task rather than the technicalities involved. See if that helps. Use the space below to record your thoughts.

Reassurance

"You are braver than you believe, stronger than you seem, and smarter than you think."

A.A. Milne.

Actors portray an image of being very confident and self-assured. The most successful people in business also portray images of self-confidence. How do they do this? They do this by telling themselves constantly they are great and can do anything they set their minds to.

When you think about it this makes sense, the best person to tell you that you are great as you are, is you. All too often we wait for other people to tell us we are great or we have done well. The only person we need to hear it from is ourselves. Why wait for someone else to tell you what you already know?

Don't be afraid to recognise the things you are good at. A good exercise is to write down a list of everything you are good at, and those things you want to improve. Make sure you write down absolutely everything you are good at. You will find there are many more things in life you excel at than you gave yourself credit for, so go ahead and celebrate your successes and the things you are good at.

Why not write down three things you would love to hear other people tell you. Now say those three things to yourself whilst looking in a mirror. How does that make you feel? Use the space below to record your thoughts.

Being the Person, you want to be

"Never complain, never explain. Resist the temptation to defend yourself or make excuses."

Brian Tracy

We should of course all celebrate the person we are and what makes us, us, but there is nothing wrong with wanting to improve ourselves, change aspects of our lives so that it makes us happier. For example, if you want to dress as a 1940s housewife and live in a 1940s themed house then why shouldn't you be that person?

There is nothing stopping anyone from being the person they want to be. In Rhonda Byrnes's book "The Secret" she talks about how people can become the person they want to be simply by projecting the image of that personality onto themselves. In other words, by thinking they are the person they want to be and acting as that person, they will become that person. We only live once and life is too short to not be the person we want to be.

SHELVE Tip

Think of the traits you admire in your heroes or heroines – write them down in the space below and ask yourself if this is the person you want to be?

Building confidence

If your confidence is not as high as you may want it to be, where do you start?

A good place to start is to see if there are any improv classes in your area. In these classes you will, with other people, act out scenes made up as you go along, this forces you to think on your toes and do or say things outside your normal comfort zone.

If you are unable to find a physical lesson, then there may be some online and it is worth searching the internet for these.

Another place to start is by using the word No. This is covered elsewhere in this book; however, the power of the word No is such that it is worth mentioning in this section as well. It is yet another example of how SHELVE can fuse different elements so that they work in harmony.

You might be the kind of person who hates to say No to anyone, you like to please people and hate letting them down. But by doing this you are placing yourself under pressure to do things you don't want to do or enjoy. Unless you say No you will not have time to do the things you want to do. The very first time you start being truthful and say No, you will find the stress of the situation will ease and you will feel relieved and more confident. The funny thing is by saying No to your requestor they will more likely have more respect for you and start treating you differently.

Look back at your notes, in the Social Section there was an exercise to say No to something, did you do this? If not, why not? Can you revisit this task or look at something else you could reject in favour of your own wellbeing?
Use the space below to record your thoughts.

Dare to do something different

"Be daring, be different, be impractical, be anything that will assert integrity of purpose and imaginative vision against the "play-it-safers", the creatures of the commonplace, the slaves of the ordinary"

Cecil Beaton

Within the Hobby section of this book, we discussed not being afraid to try and do something different but doing something different doesn't necessarily mean trying a new hobby, it could be anything. As an example, I was invited to an 80's fancy dress party last year, unfortunately, it had to be cancelled. I had planned on wearing a boring 80's type outfit, but I have now decided, I will go as the person I have always wanted to dress as – Adam Ant. It's a bold step but why shouldn't I? what have I got to lose? After all, I will be with friends. The freedom of being able to express ourselves as we want is something our previous generations fought for, and it is our individual and collective responsibility to make the most of the freedoms we have been afforded.

Look again at your notes on hobbies, and on the type of person you want to be, have you had further thoughts on how you will accomplish this? In defining the person, you want to be is there a way you want to dress to reflect who you are? Would for example dressing totally in a single colour make you feel good about yourself? Would it reflect the person you are? If you are thinking of starting a hobby are there clothes you need to buy to inspire you into the hobby? Sometimes dressing the part is the start of doing something different.

Use the space below to record your thoughts.

Part 4

Using **SHELVE** to create your Plan

"Our goals can only be reached through a vehicle of a plan, in which we must fervently believe, and upon which we must vigorously act. There is no other route to success."

Pablo Picasso

Taking Stock

Knowing what YOU want from life is different for everyone. In creating a plan to improve your life, find happiness and wellbeing, you need to know where you are starting from and where you want to be

Defining where you are

In Part 1 of this book, we looked at the SHELVE Life Wheel and an example was given on how to complete it.

On the next page is the example from Part 1, let's see how it can help us formulate a plan.

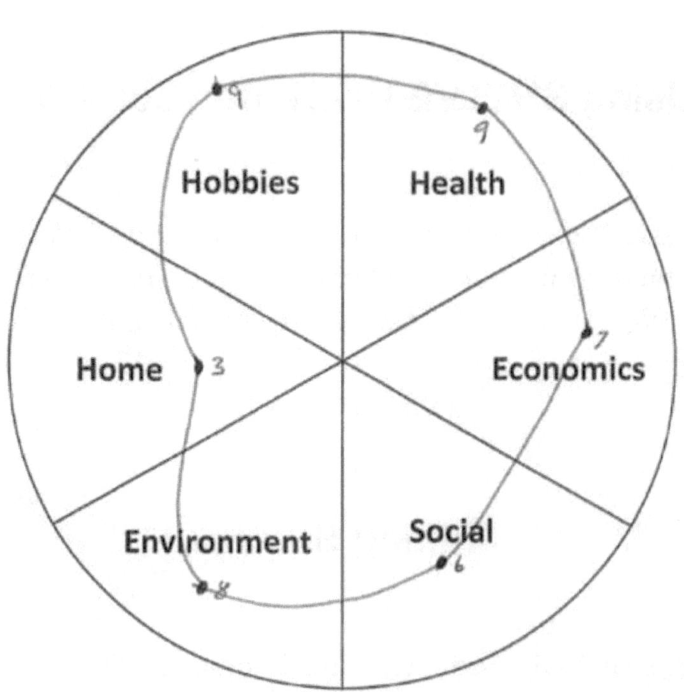

Hobbies
Health
Home
3
Economics
7
Environment
8
Social
6
9
9

Below is the Facilitator Shelve Wheel, this represents the six tools within SHELVE. Of course, you can always use tools outside of SHELVE but the purpose of these tools is they will help you focus more on incorporating Vintage Slow, Simple, Hygge, Lagom and Improv into your daily life.

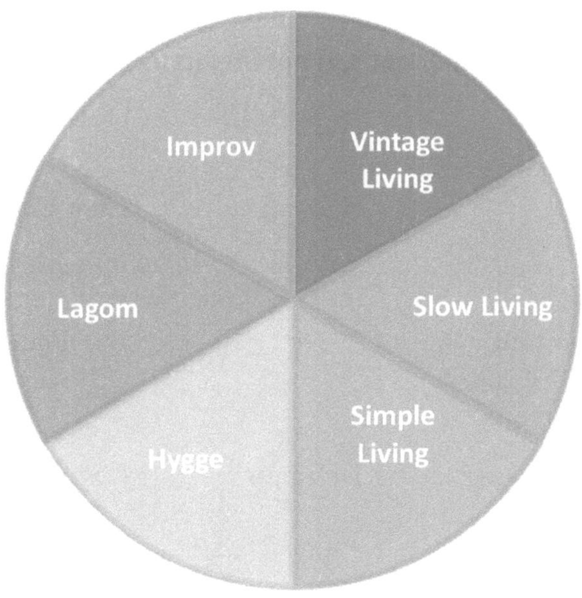

Prioritising

Highly effective and successful people are exceptionally good at prioritising their time and the tasks they take on, so they achieve maximum benefit for themselves and their organisations.

The principles are surprisingly simple and revolve around what's urgent, not urgent, important and not important.

	Urgent	Not Urgent
Important	Do	Plan
Not Important	Delegate	Eliminate

The table above shows us that if something is urgent and important then we should prioritise it as something we do now, if it is important but urgent then we should plan to do the task in the future. Things that are not important but urgent we would look to delegate to someone else and those that are not important and not urgent we can eliminate, thus clearing time to concentrate on important tasks.

Prioritising the Wheel of Life, in our example, is slightly different as there are clearly four areas that require attention. Economics, Social, Environment and Home. Depending on the detail and number of tasks within each area you could use the table above to further prioritise within each segment.

Setting Goals The SMART Way

There is a term used in business that you may have heard of, and this is the setting of SMART goals. These are goals that are Specific, Measurable, Achievable, Realistic and within Timelines or Timeframes. This type of goal setting works well and is tried and tested.

When looking at our own lives and how we want to simplify and find wellbeing, we would probably end up with a very long list. It is, therefore, better to break your goals down into categories and have a maximum of three or four goals in each category.

Too many goals are unrealistic, and you will lose sight of what it is you are trying to achieve. Too few and you lose motivation as it may be easy to achieve them and then what do you do?

A common mistake is to make goals too easy or too hard. If you see instant progress, then it is too easy, and you will be satisfied quickly when you could have made better progress overall in life with a slightly harder goal.

Too hard a goal and you will not make progress and lose motivation. That's why Diets are hard to stick to. Often a diet promises you will lose say a stone in a month. Your metabolism is slow, and you only lose a couple of pounds by week three, inevitably you will lose the motivation to see it through to week four and start eating badly again.

To set goals, you need to consider what you can realistically achieve within a given timeframe. Integral to achieving the goal is <u>how</u> you are going to do this, what actions or lifestyle changes do you need to make to achieve your goal?

Don't be afraid to change the timeframe or re-engineer your goals, what matters is you make progress and see results. This in turn motivates you.

It can be useful for goals to be interdependent as this is something else that can provide motivation.

Let's look at clarification of each element of the SMART goal:

Specific	Who, what, where, when, which, and why?
Measurable	How much, how many, how will I know when I have accomplished it?
Achievable	How am I going to make it happen, which SHELVE facilitators can I use?
Realistic	Is the goal realistic, too hard, or too easy?
Timeframe	When do I aim to achieve this, how often do I do this task?

So, for each of the life areas we want to improve, we can set a smart goal. Our overall goal is to get closer to happiness and wellbeing within six months by improving the areas of our life we are unhappy with. Here is an example of how our SMART goals would look.

SHELVE Life Area: Economics	
Specific	I wish to pay off a credit card debt of £1000 in six months.
Measurable	The amount to be paid off is £1000. When my debt is £0 I will have achieved my goal.
Achievable	I will do this by adopting a more vintage lifestyle whereby I will do my own cleaning and use eco-friendly products. I will save £40 a week which is the equivalent of £160 a month and £960 over six months.
Realistic	I can do this as I have a couple of hours spare twice a week. I can easily make up for the £40 shortfall.
Timeframe	I will do the cleaning twice a week and in six months will have paid the debt off.

SHELVE Life Area: Social	
Specific	I have just started a new job, and I don't know anyone at work. As everyone at my new job has been there a while I feel like an outsider.
Measurable	I need to buy 10 cinnamon buns and enough coffee for 10 people. I can find out specific coffee needs on the day.
Achievable	I will arrange for my work colleagues to do (Lagom) Fika, on a Friday afternoon. I will pluck up the courage by raising this as an impro*vised* idea at our next team meeting.
Realistic	We always do something on a Friday afternoon so I could suggest my Fika Coffee Break. I can buy the buns on the way to work from a local baker's and I can take orders for the coffee from the canteen.
Timeframe	Our next team meeting is a week Monday, I will suggest my Fika break for next Friday.

SHELVE Life Area: Environment	
Specific	I wish to reduce the amount of chemical cleaning products I am using.
Measurable	I want to replace the daily kitchen and bathroom sprays that I use.
Achievable	I have a Simple/Vintage Living recipe for making cleaning spray, it involves using left over lemon from my tea, vinegar and water.
Realistic	As I will not be employing a cleaner, I can make my detergent and use it when I do the cleaning.
Timeframe	It takes two weeks to make my detergent so I will make it this week, use up the old detergent and then start using it instead of buying more shop detergent.

SHELVE Life Area: Home	
Specific	I feel like I can't move in my house as I have too much stuff and I have visitors coming in a month.
Measurable	I need to clear enough space so I have room for a sofa bed so my visitors can stay.
Achievable	I will use the De-cluttering techniques found in the Simple Living section of SHELVE.
Realistic	As I only have a month and need to order the sofa bed, I shall concentrate my efforts on the spare room to start with and then move to the rest of the house.
Timeframe	I will declutter the spare room this weekend and order my sofa bed. I should then have enough time to declutter the other rooms before my guests arrive.

Creating your SHELVE Project Plan

Now that we have identified goals for each of the Life areas requiring attention, we can now put these goals into an overall plan which may look like this:

Life Area	Goal	Importance	Priority	Completion Date	Notes
Economics	Pay off CC	High	High	Six Months	Start Straight away
Social	Lagom Coffee Afternoon (Fika)	High	Low	Plan for a couple of weeks	
Environment	Cleaning	Low	High	Six Months	Will form part of Economics
Home	Declutter	High	High	One Month	Guests Staying make this urgent

The table on the previous page is just an example and helps to pull your plan together so you can see what you have to do all in one place. Note the goal in economics to save money by doing the cleaning yourself also means you have effectively delegated the Environment Task. Whilst it's not as urgent to you as the others, it is being dealt with through the Economics goal.

One of the main reasons why SHELVE works so well is the fusion between different life areas and the Facilitators. Quite often a change in one area will result in a benefit to another area. Slow, Simple and Vintage Living by their very nature environmentally friendly and financially frugal.

Having created your plan let's look at some of the things which might slow you down and some motivators to help you achieve your goals.

Negativity

"Life is too short to spend in negativity. So, I have made a conscious effort to not be where I don't want to be"

Hugh Dillon

The biggest hurdle in the way of achieving goals and positive thinking is negativity. Negative people are not only draining but they are selfish to the point they hinder the progress of people around them.

The people we associate with tend to become the people we become. If we associate with positive people, then we can't help but have some of that positivity rub off on us. Because they are upbeat and looking for the positives in life, we too become positive. It is said that if you associate with successful people then your success increases, and you too become successful. The reason behind this is that your conversations will turn to successful strategies that have worked for your friends. By associating with successful people, you are constantly picking up knowledge to help you be successful and pointers on how to avoid failure.

Associate with negative people and you too will become negative, always looking for someone else to blame because it is easier than looking at why you have failed at something.

Everyone at some point will have something negative to say about something or other, but the problem starts when people you associate with become negative about everything.

Pretty soon that rubs off and you too will find your thoughts are dominated by negative ones. For example, you leave your house in the morning and see someone has parked a large unsightly vehicle in your road, what do you think?

1. Do you let it get to you and think "that's ugly, why have they parked it there and what a nuisance it is"?
2. Do you think it's temporary and someone must be working hard to be out that early?
3. Do you ignore it and think instead of your day ahead and how nice the weather is?

Looking at the 1st option, this is likely to start winding you up and put you in a bad mood. Having been put in a bad mood the very next thing you see that annoys you will put you in an even worst mood and so on until your blood pressure is raised. But what good has that done? None, you have let yourself become negative when it could have been avoided simply through your mindset and how you view the world.

If your response was 2 or 3 then you are likely to have a much better day with less stress, and it's not cost you anything. After all, short of tracking down the owner and asking them to move it, which is likely to cause an argument, you are in a better place. The calmness allows you to enjoy the rest of your day, or at least be better placed to deal with any further annoyances.

SHELVE Tip

The next time you see something causing you to have negative thoughts, stop and re-imagine a positive spin on the situation instead.

Write down in the space below all your negative thoughts and identify those that can be turned into goals for change. For example, "I feel I am overweight" becomes "I am starting a diet on Monday"

Motivation

"All our dreams can come true, if we have the courage to pursue them"

Walt Disney

To achieve great things in life or to make ourselves content with our achievements, we need to understand we can only achieve things for ourselves by ourselves.

There is no magic formula and most people do not win the lottery. Those people who do achieve success do this because of their hard work rather than by luck.

And so it is with finding happiness and wellbeing, only you can make the future you want, no one else can do this for you.

The key to getting motivated is being in the right place mentally to start with and this is why taking care of ourselves is so important.

Most people will lose motivation through fatigue which can be caused by poor mental or physical health. The other reason why people lose motivation is because they have set themselves goals that are either too easy or too hard.

There exists a theory that in setting goals you are more likely to succeed if your goal is set in the third person. For example, your goal may be to cut down on the amount of fuel you use in your car to save money, but you are more likely to be successful if you view it as cutting down to help the environment and people around you, rather than cutting down to help yourself save money. If you find you have lost motivation, try viewing the goal in the third person.

Good Habits to get into

Steven Covey wrote a book in 1989 called "The Seven Habits of Highly Effective People"

Below is a summary of these Habits – I have tried these, and I have found them highly effective.

- Be Proactive – be the one to take the initiative
- Begin with the end in mind – if you don't know where you are going then how are you going to plan your journey?
- Put first things first. This is about prioritising and deciding what's important.
- Think Win-Win – think positive, be positive
- Seek to Understand, then to be understood – listen when people speak so that they listen to you, and you solve problems together
- Synergise – Combining the strengths of people through Teamwork
- Sharpen the Saw – constant renewal of your resources, energy, and health to create a sustainable lifestyle

A few other habits I have found particularly helpful, some of which are covered in more detail in other parts of this book:

- The importance of a proper sleep routine
- If you have many unpleasant tasks to tick off your "to-do" list, then tackle one a day until you have completed them
- Start your day slowly
- Plan your day the night before or in the morning, whichever works for you. Planning is the difference between being busy or being productive.
- Keep a diary or journal in which to record your thoughts, plans and dreams. It helps you focus your mind on what it is you want, and you can use it to measure your progress in the future
- Make sure you have at least one hobby – this helps you distance yourself from day-to-day worries, gives you time to reflect and most importantly keeps your brain challenged, particularly if you are learning new skills

We are all different and we all have many ways of finding motivation, finding what works for you and ask others what works for them.

Closing Comments and Further Resources

Now you have finished this book and have hopefully compiled your own plan to help you on your journey to finding happiness and wellbeing, you may now want to look at further resources to help you on your way.

There are several books relating to Scandinavian lifestyle choices. Amongst these are:

The Little Book of Hygge by Meil Wiking

Hygge: The Secrets of the Hygge art towards a Stress-Free and Happier Life by Danielle Kristiansen

The Hygge Activity Book for all Seasons (puzzles and activities) by Olivia Lanae

Lagom: The Swedish Art of Balanced Living by Linnea Dunne

Lagom: The Swedish Art of a Balanced, Happy Life by Niki Brantmark

Lagom: The Swedish Art of Eating Harmoniously by Steffi Knowles-Dellner

Hygge and Lagom DIY Bundle: Scandinavian Living Tips by Maya Thoresen and Nicole Scaradge

Friluftsliv: Everything you need to know about the Nordic Lifestyle Friluftsliv by Sofie Bakken

The Nordic Guide to Living Ten Years Longer by Dr Bertil Marklund

10-Minute Digital Declutter: The Simple Habit to Eliminate Technology Overload by S.J.Scott

Mindful Digital Simplicity by Andrew William James

Kinfolk – Slow Living Magazine

The Gentle Art of Swedish Death Cleaning by Margareta Magnusson

Facebook has a number of pages and communities which are friendly and helpful relating to Simple Living, Slow Living. Hygge (search for Hygge Life), Lagom you need to search for, at the time of writing there didn't appear to be a group.

Youtube has many channels relating to all of the topics in the book, some of my favourite lifestyle themed channels are Apronful of Stones, Honeyjubu, and Fairyland Cottage.

I wish you well with your journey and hope you found the topics in this book have helped you form your plan to find happiness and wellbeing.

If you have enjoyed reading this book then please leave a review.

Templates – Life Wheels

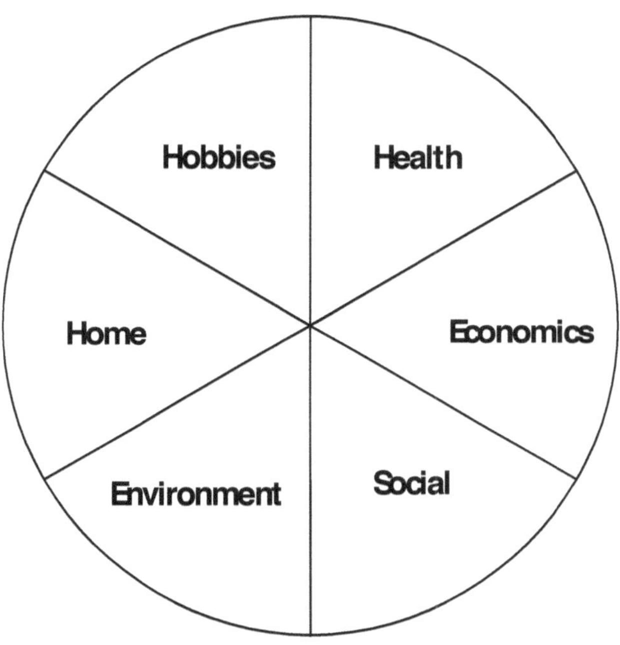

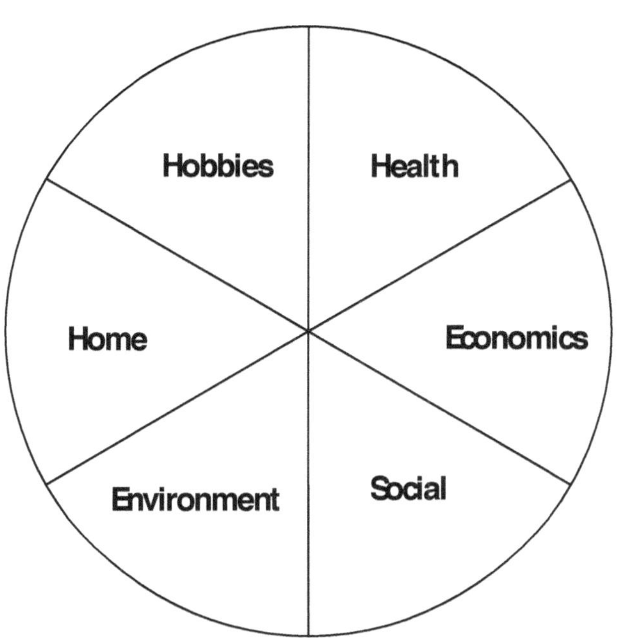

Hobbies
Health
Home
Economics
Environment
Social

Templates SMART Project Plans

SHELVE Life Area: Economics	
Specific	
Measurable	
Achievable	
Realistic	
Timeframe	

SHELVE Life Area: Social	
Specific	175
Measurable	
Achievable	
Realistic	
Timeframe	

SHELVE Life Area: Environment	
Specific	177
Measurable	
Achievable	
Realistic	
Timeframe	

SHELVE Life Area: Home	
Specific	179
Measurable	
Achievable	
Realistic	
Timeframe	

SHELVE Life Area: Health	
Specific	181
Measurable	
Achievable	
Realistic	
Timeframe	

SHELVE Life Area: Hobbies	
Specific	
Measurable	
Achievable	
Realistic	
Timeframe	

Templates – Project Plan Summary

Life Area	Goal	Impor-tance	Priority	Completion Date	Notes
Economics					
Social					
Environment					
Home					
Health					
Hobbies